D1485410

NODDY HOLDER

WHO'S CRAZEE NOW?

NODDY
HOLDER

WHO'S

CRAZEE

NOW?

MY AUTOBIOGRAPHY

WITH LISA VERRICO

EBURY
PRESS

This edition published in Great Britain in 1999

1 3 5 7 9 10 8 6 4 2

Copyright © 1999 Noddy Holder

All Rights Reserved. Used Under Authorisation.

All rights reserved. No part of this publication may be reproduced, stored in a retrieval system, or transmitted in any form or by any means, electronic, mechanical, photocopying, recording or otherwise, without prior permission from the copyright owners

Ebury Press
Random House, 20 Vauxhall Bridge Road, London SW1V 2SA

Random House Australia Pty Limited
20 Alfred Street, Milsons Point, Sydney, New South Wales 2061, Australia

Random House New Zealand Limited
18 Poland Road, Glenfield, Auckland 10, New Zealand

Random House South Africa (Pty) Limited
Endulini, 5A Jubilee Road, Parktown 2193, South Africa

The Random House Group Limited. Reg. No. 954009

A CIP catalogue record for this book is available from the British Library

ISBN: 0 09 187075 5

Extract from 'Far Far Away' courtesy Barn Publishing (Slade) Ltd.

Cover design by Jamie Keenan
Photo section design by Blackjacks

Photographs © credited copyright holders.
All other photographs private collection of Noddy Holder.

Typeset by SX Composing DTP, Rayleigh, Essex
Printed and bound in Great Britain by Biddles of Guildford

Papers used by Ebury Press are natural, recyclable products made from wood grown in sustainable forests.

I've seen the yellow lights go down the Mississipi

I've seen the bridges of the world and they're for real

I've had a red light off the wrist

Without me even getting kissed

It still seems so unreal

I've seen the morning in the mountains of Alaska

I've seen the sun set in the east and in the west

I've sang the glory that was Rome

And passed the Hound Dog singer's home

It all seems for the best

And I'm far far away . . .

THE

BOY

CAN'T HELP

IT

1

I'm standing centre-stage, faces staring up at me in the darkness of a dimly lit room, the heat from the lights above adding to the nervous perspiration pouring down my forehead. My heart is pumping so hard, it could burst out of my chest. My hands, holding the microphone, are shaking as my vocal chords work flat out on the current No.1 record in the charts. The year is 1953, the venue is Walsall Labour Club and the song is Frankie Laine's 'I Believe'. This was my debut singing in front of a live audience. I was seven years old and there wasn't a dry eye in the house.

I was born being rowdy – or so my mum says. I kicked like mad in the womb and was screaming when I hit daylight. I suppose it was my first spotlight and I'm a great believer in starting as you mean to go on. I do believe there's such a thing as a 'born performer', that there's something in you that gives you the confidence to entertain. It's more than showing off – it's following the dream.

My dad came from a big family and my mum had a sister, so there were lots of aunts and uncles and cousins. We were always at one anothers' houses. It was the same with the neighbours – loads of kids to play with, so even though I had no brothers or sisters, I was never bored. But the absence of siblings did help turn me towards my own talents at a very early age. I would often go into my own little world. I'd create fantasies and stories in my head, only to be interrupted by my mum shouting, 'Neville, your dinner's ready.' I'm the same today, often trying to grab an hour on my own. When I was in bands and on tour, I'd take time out in the dressing room, sit alone in a corner and focus on the show ahead. As frontman, I'd be concentrating on going over things that might go wrong, the chats with the audience between songs, new ideas – anything to make sure the show went smoothly. Doing this, with mayhem going on all around, made me seem shut-off and moody. But most other times, I'd be at the centre of the action, causing all the chaos. It confused the hell out of people. So be it.

My memory of childhood is a totally happy one. We were a typical working-class family, where parents simply couldn't afford to spoil their kids. Rationing carried on from the war until 1954 and there was never any excess money anyway. No one saved much. You lived from day to day. That said, I don't ever remember us being totally skint, although I'm sure that information was kept from us kids. It just wasn't any of our business. In our house there was always food on the table and a coal fire in the living room.

I was an end-of-the-war baby, born at 8am on Saturday, 15 June 1946 at Number 31½ Newhall Street in Walsall. Don't ask me to explain the 'and-a-half' business. I've no idea what it meant, but I always thought that extra half made a difference. Walsall is just north of Birmingham and part of the Black Country, so called because for years it had been the industrial heartland of England. When I was a lad, there were still thriving coal mines, iron and steel foundries and factories with huge chimneys billowing smoke, which left sooty deposits everywhere. It really was Black Country by name and Black Country by nature! I'm extremely proud of my Midlands roots. Black Country folk truly are the salt of the earth and without them, I would not be able to speak 'as proppa as wot I do'.

Our council house was at the end of a long terrace. The opening credits of *Coronation Street* always remind me of Newhall Street. The layout of all the houses was pretty much the same. The front door opened directly on to the pavement and you walked straight into the front room, which was only used on special occasions. My mum said it was 'to be kept for best' – many things were 'kept for best' in those days. You then passed into the living room, where there was a dining table and chairs and a couple of armchairs around a big black coal-fire stove. A huge black kettle, full of hot water, would always be resting there. There was no central heating with constant hot water on tap in those days, my friends. The living room was also the setting for my Friday night scrub-down in an old tin bath. A sideboard completed the picture and, of course, there was a wireless – that's the radio to anyone born after 1960.

A door opening on to the stairs took you up to two bedrooms. There was no bathroom or indoor toilet. If you were caught short during the night, you used a chamber pot under the bed. A good aim was crucial in these circumstances. In the bitter cold of winter you cuddled up in bed under layers of blankets with a hot water bottle. Today, all my family complain that I don't have the central heating up high enough. It must be a roll-over from those days – but I'm a naturally hot-blooded kind of guy.

Downstairs, the room at the back of the house had a gas stove and a large sink where clothes were scrubbed clean by hand. The backyard was shared with three other families and the only toilet was at the end of the yard, with a bolt on the inside of a rickety wooden door. It was quite a trek for a little kid just to have a crap! Sheets of newspaper hung on a hook for the ceremonial wiping and luckily in those days print didn't come off the paper. A Daily Mirror headline smeared across your backside would not have been a pretty sight.

1945 was a very good year. The war ended, the survivors came home and I was conceived. My dad, Jack, had been away for six years, serving with Montgomery's Desert Rats and in Italy. He had lost a huge chunk of his youth and the experience had affected him deeply. He'd never really talk about those times though, not unless he'd had too much to drink. But he always insisted I go with him every

Remembrance Sunday to the Cenotaph in the town centre to watch the parade and honour the dead. The war left him with a passionate hatred of Germans, which I suppose is understandable, because many of his mates never came back. I didn't fully grasp how much of an impression the war had left on him until much later in life. His true feelings surfaced when I had a German girlfriend for a while. Once she came over to England to visit. I was still living at home with mum and dad, so she stayed with us. My dad couldn't bring himself to utter more than a few words to her the whole time she was there. It was a shame, because she hadn't even been born in Germany.

Generally, I was well-behaved as a child. At least I was when I needed to be. It wasn't just because I knew I'd get flak from my dad if I wasn't. Kids back then ran amok less than they do today. Society conspired to keep you in line. At school you got the cane at the first sign of disorderly behaviour. You'd get it on your hands or your arse, which bloody hurt, so it put you off being too bad. Teachers were figures of authority and they could give you a good whacking as often as they liked. They didn't have to ask your parents first either. In fact, if you were caught misbehaving, most parents would positively encourge them to discipline you. We spent our school years actually frightened of our headmistress. We were terrified of policemen too and it didn't help that my dad knew all the cops. He knew everyone. He was a window-cleaner with his own business, which meant he did all the neighbours' houses, local shops, factories, police stations, schools, all sorts. He was quite a character. He'd be out in the street chatting to people while he was working. It wasn't an easy life though, not by any means. He had to leave home at the crack of dawn every day. In his later years, he had terrible arthritis from being outside for hours on end in all sorts of weather. He was a real grafter, no doubt about it.

Both my grandads had died before I was born, but I remember visiting my nans' houses every week. My mum's mum had this fantastic piano. Most families had a piano in the house, but hers was real fancy. It had candlesticks and bits of inlaid ivory. It was hardly ever played, but it was always perfectly in tune. Even at the age of two or three, I'd always plonk myself in front of it and bang away at the keys for hours and hours. To this day, it's one of my big regrets in life that I never learnt to play the piano properly.

There's no doubt I was a show-off from an early age. I was four when I gave my first public performance. It was with my puppet theatre. My uncle Eric had built it for me and I would put on shows in our backyard for other kids and charge them one old penny each to come along. I used to write my own plays for the puppets, basically my versions of Punch and Judy stories. Then I would act them out like I was some sort of professional entertainer, which I guess I thought I was.

Later, when I got bored with puppets, I turned my attention to music. The wireless became my main distraction. Whenever I heard a particular song that I liked, I would learn all the lyrics. Then I'd stand in the yard with a broomstick for a mic and sing them over and over. The wireless I really remember was my nan's. She had one of those ancient models which was powered by what was called an accumulator. It was like a car battery. It had to be taken to a shop once or twice a week to be charged. I always wanted to carry it, but it was too heavy for me. Radio played a big part in family life in those days, because hardly anyone had a television, not where we lived anyway. Kids would sit with their parents listening to the wireless, to shows like Educating Archie, Life with the Lyons and The Clitheroe Kid. There were no arguments over music, because you only ever heard whatever were the popular songs of the day. Radio stations didn't always play the actual records though. Instead, they brought in various dance-bands to perform a selection of hits.

A big boost of my fledgling singing career came the day that my dad arrived home with our first radiogram, which was a record player and radio built into one. It was a huge piece of furniture, driven by valves. Of course, I was thrilled. It's hard to imagine today, but being able to play your favourite songs whenever you liked was incredibly exciting. It certainly made it easier for me to learn lyrics. I was lucky because my dad began buying lots of records straight away. I remember the very first record we got. It was 'Via Con Dias' by The Beverley Sisters, which was popular at the time. My dad's favourite artist was probably Al Jolson, which rubbed off on me. To this day, I'm still a Jolson fan.

It never occurred to me at the time, but most of my family were musical in their own way. Dad's elder brother used to sing, mum played the violin as a kid and her sister played the piano. I remember that my mum's violin was always in its case somewhere around the house, though she only played it occasionally. She'd either grown out of it by the time I was born or she was just too busy to bother with it any more. I was aware that my dad had musical talent too. He had a great voice and he used to sing around the house all the time. His favourite song was 'You Made Me Love You', which I think was originally sung by Judy Garland. It was his party piece – he'd sing it to mum when he came home pissed from the pub. He sang it in public too, in the working men's clubs. Every couple of weeks, he would get up on stage and belt out a few numbers. People often said he could have been a professional singer, because he always went down a storm.

In the '50s, working men's clubs were part of the community, places of entertainment where parents would go with their kids once or twice a week, usually on a Friday or Saturday night. Our local was Walsall Labour Club, which was right in the centre of town. Downstairs was a room with snooker tables, which I remember thinking looked absolutely huge but were probably just regular size. It was only the men who played snooker. I'd run around the tables when my dad was playing. I loved to collect the balls from the pockets and put them back on their spots. I thought of it as my special job. I tried to look after the balls on every table at the same time. I thought I was being a big help, but I was probably more of a nuisance. Upstairs at the club, there was a bar, lots of tables and chairs and a stage where various acts would perform at weekends. Part of the show was called 'free and easy'. It was when anyone in the audience could get up and play the piano or sing. I reckon it was on that stage that the entertainment bug hit me.

After making my debut there, I became a regular, singing whatever big pop hits of the day I knew. Sometimes I'd get up and do a duet with my cousin Pauline, who was a bit older than me. Mostly though, I'd sing on my own. I don't think any other kids my age ever performed and I'm pretty sure my parents didn't push me into it. I wanted to be up there. I had heard the audience cheering when they liked an act and it gave me a buzz. I imagined how great it would be to get that reception myself.

During the week, my dad would go out with his mates. All the blokes went down the boozer, while their wives were at home cooking the tea. They'd come back drunk, expecting to be fed. That was the working-class way and we were no different. Women just didn't go to the pub without their husbands. It they did, they were thought of as flighty. In that day and age, all men liked to drink. For my dad, it was probably his greatest pleasure in life – well, that and going to the bookies to bet on the horses or the greyhounds. He was mad on sport, any sport. He particularly loved football – he supported Wolverhampton Wanderers and Walsall. I'd go to the match with him now and again, but mainly we went to the cricket together. We used to go as a family on a Saturday afternoon, because Walsall Cricket ground was only a ten-minute walk from our house, in the posh part of town. In fact, cricket became quite a ritual with us. We went to the away games as well. The three of us would catch the bus to wherever a match was on, because my dad didn't drive then.

The thing that always sticks in my mind about going to the cricket was that everyone in the crowd always sat in the same seats. Each week you'd be surrounded by the same faces. It was like that in working men's clubs too. We always sat at the same table, in the same seats, as did everyone else in the room. It was part of the reason that you rarely met anyone you didn't already know. If a new family moved into the area, it was quite a big deal, although within a week they would have made friends with the whole community. Compared to today, it really was an incredibly insular way of life. People lived in each other's pockets. Neighbours would constantly pop unannounced into any house in the street. You didn't lock your back door and you knew everybody's business. Even when you went on holiday, you were likely to meet the neighbours, or at least the same families you'd seen the year before.

No one we knew ever went abroad. If we were lucky we'd go to Rhyl or Margate for a week. On the few occasions that we were very adventurous, we went to Torquay which was a bit further away. Families only had one week's holiday a year in those days, so they tended to go wherever they could get to quickly. In our case, the nearest seaside resorts were all in North Wales.

Looking back, I can't think of a single way in which my parents weren't totally typical of their working-class generation. Everyone we knew was happy with their lot. As long as you had work, your sport and you could go for a drink, you considered yourself lucky. It seemed that everyone in the community felt that way – well, everyone except me. I did enjoy my childhood, but I always had the feeling that I was destined for a different future. I remember there was a huge posh park in Sutton Coldfield, just on the outskirts of Birmingham, where I sometimes went with my mates at the weekend. To get there we took the bus, then walked through this amazing area where all the rich people lived. I always told myself that as soon as I earned enough money, I'd buy one of those houses. I did too, although it was many many years later.

When I was eight, my family moved from the terraced house to a newly-built council estate called Beechdate. Our old street was due to be demolished, so everyone had to be rehoused. We were the first to go though. I think it was because our house was at the end of the block and in the worst state of disrepair. Unfortunately, no one thought to move all the families together, so I lost a lot of my old friends. As a kid, it was quite an unsettling experience. I stayed at the same school, but rather than being able to walk there, I had to make a long journey on the bus every day. Our new place was on the opposite side of town, in the middle of fields and surrounded by pools where you could go fishing. In later years, we used to ride over the nearby hills on motorbikes. I had new places to explore and new kids to meet. It felt like the biggest thing that had ever happened to me.

To be honest, if I had been forced to move to a new school too, I don't think I would have minded much. I went to a Church of England infants and junior school, not because my family was particularly religious, but simply because it was the closest to us, at least it was when I started there. The main church in Walsall was St Matthew's and the school, which was called Walsall Blue Coat, was connected to that. Some of the kids at the school were from posher families and I found their backgrounds a bit intimidating. I never felt comfortable around them. When I went to birthday parties at their posh houses, I couldn't believe my eyes. It was like another world. I found it hard to understand why some people lived like that and we didn't.

I vaguely recall being picked on in the playground a couple of times. It was because of my size. I was a tiny kid. Physically I took after my mum, who was very small and slender, although I did have my dad's features and his thick wavy hair. I would never say I was bullied though. I caught on pretty quickly that if you could make people laugh, they thought you had bottle and left you alone. It was a case of putting the natural performer in me to good use.

I was christened Neville John Holder and at infants school, I got my first nickname – Neville the Devil – but the nickname that stuck for good came at junior school. A boy in my class called John Robbins gave it to me when I was

11

seven. He started calling me Noddy. I never really knew why. I just assumed it was because I always nodded in lessons instead of saying 'yes'. It stuck straight away and I never gave it a second thought. It wasn't until years later, when I was famous, that someone asked me about it. I got so used to everyone calling me Noddy. It was only my mum, my aunties and my teachers at school who ever called me Neville. I even introduced myself as Noddy. I didn't prefer one or the other, I was just Noddy.

By far the most exciting day at junior school was when a kid called John Taylor told me the fact of life. I used to sit beside him in the back row of class. His dad was a Scout leader and he'd been a Scout himself for years. For some reason that had helped him find out about sex. I'm not sure why, but it had just made him more worldly wise. In those days, sex wasn't a subject you were told much about. Even teenagers were incredibly naive by today's standards. You were just expected to fumble through and work things out in your own way. Parents would rather have died than sit down and talk about the birds and the bees. I had inklings of how it happened, but I was flabbergasted when John filled me in on the details. It didn't make me want to join the Scouts though.

In the '50s, most people went to the cinema at least a couple of times a week. In Walsall alone there were four or five little picture houses. There aren't any now, just the multiplexes outside town. Like all kids my age, I grew up with Saturday morning cinema. I'd go with a couple of lads from our street at 9.30am each week. We'd watch a cowboy film featuring Hopalong Cassidy or the Cisco Kid and maybe a Flash Gordon episode, one of the original black-and-white ones. I particularly remember my early trips to the cinema because, on the way there, I had to walk past the post office. For some reason, it had toys for sale and in the window was an electric train set – all set up and fully working. I had never seen anything like it. I could stand for hours and watch that train go round the track.

By the time we moved to the new estate, I was old

enough to go to the cinema in the early evenings. At first, I went with friends from school or the neighbours' kids. Then I started going on my own. I thought it was great being independent. Moving house had made me a lot more confident, because I was having to travel across town on the bus every day. I thought that going to see a movie on my own was a very grown-up thing to do.

I was nine when I saw my first rock 'n' roll film. It was Rock Around the Clock with Bill Haley and it blew my mind. Rock 'n' roll had only just crossed the Atlantic and Bill Haley and The Comets were our first taste of the American Dream. I went to see the movie on my own at a matinee at the local cinema. It was the Teddy Boy era and the news was full of stories about teenagers causing trouble. I had heard that at screenings of Rock Around the Clock, kids were ripping out the cinema seats and jiving in the aisles. My parents had heard that too and had told me I couldn't go. I nicked some of my dad's Brylcream, slicked back my hair and went anyway – the urge was irresistible. I don't think I even asked any of my mates to come. I knew they wouldn't be interested. They weren't into music, no one my age was. As it turned out, there was no trouble at all, just lots of excitement. It was fantastic for me to see all these teenagers dancing and singing along to the songs. I didn't join in because I was the only kid in the place. I just watched it all going on, totally wide-eyed.

From that day on, anything with a rock 'n' roll sound-track was good as far as I was concerned. I even went to see all the Tommy Steele films, although I wasn't particularly a fan of his music. Tommy Steele was a huge star back then, the pop idol of the day. He sang cover versions of American hits. When Elvis and Little Richard came along, I realised they were the real thing! Their films were much more hard-hitting and gritty. Simply the fact that they were American made them seem more exciting.

I'll never forget the day I saw Little Richard on screen for the first time. He was in The Girl Can't Help It . I didn't think rock 'n' roll could get any better than that. There he was, banging away on the piano with his bouffant hair. To me, he was the coolest man alive. A few years later, I got to see Little Richard in concert. He came to the Gaumont in Wolverhampton on a package tour with The Rolling Stones, who were the opening act, and The Everly Brothers, who were top of the bill. This was my first big rock 'n' roll show. It was mind-blowing. I flipped out over Little Richard in particular, probably because he was so flamboyant. He danced on top of the piano and threw himself around the stage. In those days, nobody knew he was gay. It seems obvious now, but it was unheard of for entertainers to come out of the closet back then. Right after Little Richard, I got into Elvis. I first saw him on screen in Jailhouse Rock and then in King Creole.

Not long after I discovered rock 'n' roll, I started saving up for my own records. The first one I bought with my own money was Larry Williams' 'Bony Moronie'. Records were all I ever wanted for birthday or Christmas presents. I had a window-cleaning round by then and all the money I made went on music. Listening to rock 'n' roll records was so exciting. It made me feel good. Somehow, even then, I knew that was my future. When I eventually got my own gramophone, I would just sit in my room for hours on end listening to all my favourite 78s. Then I began to imagine how great it would be if I could actually play those sounds myself. That's when I decided to get a guitar. In the '50s, the guitar wasn't the popular instrument it is today. Elvis may have made it the symbol of rock 'n' roll, but round our way no kid actually owned one. I got my first guitar at the age of twelve. My parents bought it for me as a Christmas present, although I was already saving up for the same one myself. It was a battered old thing, not even electric, from a secondhand shop not far from our house. I had seen it in the window dozens of times, because I walked past the shop every day to catch the bus back from school. I had fallen in love with it the first time I saw it, but it cost £3 which was a lot of money to a kid back then. I couldn't believe my eyes when my parents gave it to me. I thought it was the greatest

Christmas present in the world. I had no idea how to play it though. Luckily my mum knew a great jazz guitarist in Walsall, Freddie Degville, who had been in bands all his life. When she saw how much that guitar meant to me, she asked him to give me a few lessons.

My first year playing guitar coincided with Cliff Richard's rise to fame. I wanted to learn all his songs. He was the British bad boy of rock, though it's hard to believe now. He came to fame on a television show called Oh Boy!, which had taken over from 6.5 Special as the pop music show. Over the years I was glued to all music shows and every Saturday teatime, I'd be there to see Cliff, Marty Wilde, Billy Fury, Adam Faith, Dickie Pride and Joe Brown. Then it would be straight up to the bedroom, collar turned up, practising the new gyrations that were part and parcel of an aspiring pop star – the reflection in the mirror, the new God's gift to the female population!

Besides Saturday-night television, my only other source of new music was weekend radio. Although rock 'n' roll had made a big impact, most radio music was still big bands covering hits of the day. As far as I remember, the only two radio shows that played my kind of music were Brian Matthews' Saturday Club on Saturday mornings and Easy Beat on Sundays. Every teenager listened to those shows. It was almost a ritual. The only station that played pop records all the time was Radio Luxembourg, but that was on very late at night and the reception was always terrible. I did sometimes try to listen to Radio Luxembourg, but it meant sneaking the wireless into my bed when I was supposed to be asleep and putting up with this awful crackling noise.

STOP THAT

?!!

RACKET!

2

By the time I got to secondary school, I was already dreaming of a future in music. I still kept up with my classes, though. I was clever and I did well in most subjects. At the end of primary, I had sat my 11-plus. That was an exam all kids took to assess what sort of secondary education they got. If you passed – which I did – you went to a grammar school. I was pleased that I had done well because I knew my parents would be proud, but even then I thought that exams were a load of nonsense. I don't think anyone should be judged on their performance at the age of eleven.

I was at the grammar school for just one year. For some reason, it was closed down after that. All the pupils were moved to a brand new school called T.P. Riley. It was one of the first comprehensives in the country. I didn't mind much what school I went to. The good thing about T.P. Riley was that it was in Bloxwich, which was only a ten-minute walk from my house. That meant I no longer had to catch the bus every day. Going there turned out to be quite an eye-opener for me. Because it was so big, it took in all the kids from our area. I couldn't believe it when I went in on the first day of term. Not only were there thousands of kids, but most of them had the same background as me. For the first time, I didn't feel out of place because I was working-class.

At the end of my second year at the comprehensive, I made friends with a kid in the year below me called Phil Burnell. We met on the very last day of term. Classes were over and everyone was told to bring in a game or an instrument or whatever, just to mess around with. Phil and I were the only ones to turn up with a guitar. We sat at opposite sides of the room, watching each other for a while. We were trying to work out which one of us was better. Eventually, I went over to talk to him. He was really small and skinny with a bowl haircut. I don't remember the first thing I said to him, but it was probably, 'How many chords do you know then?' We got chatting and found out that we liked the same records. We were both at a similar standard on the guitar too, although I may have been a bit more advanced than he was. Straight away, we formed a bond. We became instant best mates. He was the only person my age I could talk to who was as besotted by music as me.

That summer, Phil and I met up almost every day to practise the guitar. All we wanted to do was learn more and more rock'n'roll tunes. Playing with someone else was good for both of us. We could teach each other what we knew and it made us determined to improve. It was also great to finally have someone to swop records with. We used to sit and chat about what records we were going to buy and how great we'd be when we'd saved up enough money to get proper guitars. We were so naive. We thought that if we got good instruments, we'd automatically become great players. We later found out it doesn't work like that.

Phil and I only lived ten minutes apart, so would spend hours at each other's houses, discussing our favourite artists and what we liked about them. We went to the cinema together too, to see rock'n'roll films, of course. By the time we started back at school, we had come to a decision. We were forming our own band.

The plan was that I would sing and play lead guitar and Phil would play rhythm guitar. At first, my dual role was a bit of a problem. I did want to be the singer, but I couldn't work out how to play and sing at the same time. I think everyone finds that tricky. It's all about co-ordination, a bit like learning to ride a bike. It seems really hard at the start, then suddenly you get it and it becomes second nature. I remember the first song I mastered. It was 'Cathy's Clown' by the Everly Brothers. That was a real breakthrough for me. From then on, everything just clicked into place.

As soon as I could sing *and* play, Phil and I began recruiting band members. We were very choosy about it. 'We shouldn't just ask our mates to join,' I told Phil. 'We only want people who like music as much as we do.' That wasn't easy. At the time, there were no other bands in our school. There was one lad in my class, Roy Brown, who was a great guitarist, but he was already in a group called The Redcaps with a bunch of older boys from outside school. I don't know how he had got so good at such a young age, but his big brother was the singer in The Redcaps, so that probably had something to do with it.

The first person to join our band was a classmate of mine called Mick Aulton. He became our drummer. His kit was a big old scout drum with one snare and a cymbal. Our original bassist was a guy called Kenny Holland. When he dropped out after a while, we replaced him with Pete Bickley, who was in Phil's year. We completed the line-up with a second singer, a big fat bloke called John 'Tubby' Cooper. Visually, Tubby was fantastic, a real jolly lad and a total showman. He also had a great voice, despite the fact that when he spoke he had a stutter. It was incredible to see him perform. In class, he often had trouble getting his sentences out. As soon as he got on stage, he totally changed.

Our idea was that Tubby would sing all the poppier songs and I would stick with the grittier stuff. His voice suited simpler upbeat songs and mine was naturally more rock'n'roll. From day one, we had a clear idea of how we wanted to sound. We took it all very seriously too, although none of us had ever been in a band before. Looking back, we must have made a right racket. Our set-up was so basic. We didn't have a single decent instrument between the five of us and we were all sharing the same amp.

*

21

For the first year or so, we called ourselves The Phantoms. We would get together once or twice a week to rehearse. We started off with songs that Phil and I already knew how to play. The others learnt their parts by ear as we went along or worked them out later at home. Mostly, we did Shadows instrumentals and well-known rock'n'roll hits. We covered Gene Vincent, Eddie Cochran, the Everly Brothers, Little Richard, whoever. In those days, no bands wrote their own material. It didn't even cross our minds to try writing an original song. We wouldn't have known where to start.

We weren't allowed to rehearse in school and as our equipment didn't take up that much space, we usually practised in one of our houses. Often it was at Phil's, because his mum didn't seem to mind us using her front room. My mum was okay for the first hour or so, but after that she'd start shouting, 'Stop that bloody racket, boys.' It was a bit off-putting. Other times, we met at our local youth club in Bloxwich, which was basically a village hall. Youth clubs were a big deal back then, because there were so few activities for kids to do. They were where you went to chase birds or meet up with mates from other schools. No one minded us setting up our gear in a corner and practising, while people played table tennis or just sat and chatted around us. Those nights at the youth club were really our first gigs. As we got better, kids would gather round and request songs. When we saw that happening, we started going to other youth clubs as well, except there we would pretend we were a proper act and ask for some money. At our local club, we only got paid if it was an actual dance night, even though we had quite a good reputation in the area by then.

It wasn't long after we made a name for ourselves in the youth clubs that we started getting gigs in pubs and working men's clubs. You had to be pretty good to play those places. They wouldn't stand for a bunch of kids rehearsing. It was around that time that we ditched the name The Phantoms. Although we were still doing some

Elvis, Little Richard and Shadows hits, we had begun playing a lot more R'n'B stuff like Chuck Berry and Muddy Waters. 'We need a more American-sounding name,' I told Phil. 'We need something that will better suit our set.' The pair of us spent a whole evening thinking up new names. By the next day, we had become The Memphis Cut-Outs.

One of our first pub shows was at The Three Men in a Boat, which was on the corner of the estate where I lived. From then on, every time we got a proper gig, we learned a few new numbers. You were never too sure what the crowd on the night was going to be like and we always tried to adapt our set to suit their taste. We could do R'n'B, rock'n'roll, pop, instrumentals, whatever they wanted. I'm sure that's why we did well from so early on. At least once a week, we got a booking somewhere, be it in a pub, a working men's club or at a school dance. We also started to play weddings and birthday parties. We took whatever we were offered. Pretty soon, we were getting three or four gigs a week, usually over the weekend. We even had a few local residencies on Saturday nights or Sunday lunchtimes.

Our parents never worried about us playing in pubs. One of them always had to drive us anyway, to take our equipment there and back. Often, a group of them would come along to watch. They were all great pals and if the gig was on a weekend, it was like a night out for them. It was good to have them in the crowd because they were all very encouraging, although I'm sure none of them ever imagined we might one day become professional musicians. They looked on it as just a hobby. As soon as we came off stage, they'd say things like, 'You were great tonight, boys' or 'The woman at the next table loved that ballad you did'.

It helped that we were making some money from the gigs. It was never very much – maybe £5 or £10 a night – which was peanuts really, but at least our parents thought we were doing something productive. We never saw any profit. Every penny we made was ploughed back into the band. It went on buying new instruments and strings for the guitars or on paying off the HP on the amps. We were gradually upgrading our equipment. I think that by then even the bassist had his own amp, which we thought was pretty impressive. I had bought a new guitar. My old one was semi-acoustic with a pick-up I had fitted myself to make it electric. The new one was loads better. It looked like a Fender. Really, it was only a cheap Hofner – there was no way I could have afforded a Fender – but it did the job.

From the start, I knew that our band was good. Almost all of the bands on the same circuit as us were a lot older, but we went down just as well, if not better than most of them. We may have got away with murder on a few occasions because of our age, but we were always rebooked. I don't remember us ever dying a death. We had a lot to put up with too. We played in some rough pubs and it wasn't unusual for a fist-fight to break out midway through our set. In fact, it was a regular occurrence in some places. We would just carry on playing. We got used to it. It was always the same people fighting, usually at the same time of night and over the same things they had argued about the week before. That was just the way some people let off steam. It stood us in good stead for the future though. In later years, we had to put up with our audiences brawling and ripping out seats. Several times, I'd be standing on stage, midway through a song, feeling as though I was watching a Wild West show, only with tables and chairs as ammunition.

By the time we were getting regular pub gigs, I not only knew that our group was good, I knew that I was good too. That gave me a lot of confidence. My personality totally changed. I had never been shy, but I became quite stroppy and very go-getting. I didn't stand for any shit from other kids. I guess you could say I turned into a bit of a jack-the-lad. I felt comfortable with myself because I knew I had found my niche in life. By that time though, I wasn't too bothered about hanging out with gangs of friends. I was closest to the guys in the band and when I wasn't with them, I spent a lot of my spare time on my own with my guitar.

When I did go out, it was usually to youth clubs or dances. Sometimes on a Saturday night, if I wasn't playing and my parents were out at the pub, a few of my mates would come round. Like most kids, as soon as we discovered alcohol, things started to get a bit rowdy. I had a couple of parties at my house, but I was always careful not to piss off my parents. When I was at someone else's house, it was a different story. I remember the first time I got really drunk. I would have been about fourteen. I used to drink the odd bottle of beer or Guinness, but that night I was on dark rum and blackcurrant juice, which was a really trendy drink in the '60s. I loved the taste of it and was guzzling it down like pop. Afterwards, I was really ill. Luckily, I was at a mate's house and his parents were away. All I remember was the room spinning round, then crashing out on the floor.

My other diversion was girls. I had two or three girl-friends at secondary school. They were really just friends who I'd meet up with at the youth club or take to the cinema at weekends. The only serious relationship I had was with a girl in my class called Christina Walker. She was my first true love. I was stuck on her, no doubt about it. She was beautiful, very tall and blonde and curvaceous. All the lads at our school fancied her. I can't remember how I ended up going out with her, because she generally only dated blokes a couple of years older. I think I may have got talking to her in the clubs. She was an amateur dancer. She used to perform in the same working men's clubs as us, so I'd bump into her sometimes at gigs. I remember being terribly jealous every time someone chatted her up. Whenever we were out, there were always blokes chasing her. We both left school at around the same time, and soon after drifted apart. That broke my heart. She broke my heart. She was the first one.

On the evenings when I wasn't playing my own gigs, I went to see as many other groups as I could. Probably the band I saw most often was The Redcaps, the one that Roy Brown from my class at school was in. I had got quite pally with him. I was also mates with two of the older members of the band, twins called Mick and Dave Walker, who were both brilliant musicians. The Redcaps were already playing big ballrooms when we were starting out, so they were great for giving us all sorts of advice. This was just prior to the Liverpool explosion and The Redcaps were playing alongside the likes of The Beatles and Gerry and The Pacemakers before they made it. What made their band special for me was the fact that their guitarist was my age. It seemed unbelievable that one of my classmates had already reached that level of success. It made me think that one day I could be there too. That was my ambition. It never occurred to me that I might do even better, that I might even turn professional. I didn't think beyond the local scene.

The two main music venues in Walsall were Bloxwich Baths and the Town Hall. The bigger-name acts always played the Town Hall, although a lot of groups who later became famous started out at the baths. I saw Shane Fenton and The Fentones there, before Shane became Alvin Stardust. Screaming Lord Sutch and His Savages played there all the time too. Loads of great musicians went through that band, like Ritchie Blackmore who went on to Deep Purple. Screaming Lord Sutch was a big influence on me. When I saw him, I realised how exciting live music could be. We were still playing youth clubs at the time, but I knew that with better equipment, in better venues, I could be just as good.

Another artist who had a huge impact on me at that time was Joe Brown. Today, he's thought of as a very middle-of-the-road artist, but back then, he was a real rock'n'roller. His guitar playing was incredible and I spent weeks trying to copy his style. In those days, kids either tried to play like Hank Marvin, who had a very echoey sound, or they wanted to be a raw raunchy guitarist like Joe Brown or Mick Green from Johnny Kidd and The Pirates. Those were the only two choices you had. I often performed Cliff and

The Shadows-type material in the band, because that's what a lot of our audiences wanted to hear, but my passion was always for the raw R'n'B players.

Probably the first important lesson I learned from watching other bands was how to act like a star. I realised early on that attitude was all, so I approached every gig, no matter what size the venue, as if we were playing Madison Square Garden. Everyone in the band did the same. That sounds ridiculous, but it's true. We acted big-time, even though there was often less than a hundred people in the audience. We thought of ourselves as professional artists and we were incredibly self-disciplined. We studied everything we liked about our favourite bands and copied not only how they were on stage, but how they behaved the rest of the time too. We wouldn't set the gear up in front of the audience, for example, because none of the bands we liked did that. They didn't hang around by the bar before a show, so neither did we. It was all about the first impression you made walking on stage.

Something else I sussed was that the clever bands made their presentation part of the performance. The crowd always went mad when a group walked on stage looking special. It was their clothes in particular which could really make an impact. The way a band dressed could give them an element of surprise. Once we'd sussed out that, we never once played in our street gear. Even when we had no money, we managed to come up with a band outfit of one sort or another. They were basically cheaper versions of what we really wanted. It was such a simple idea, but so effective. If you won an audience over with a look, you were halfway to getting them on your side before playing a single note. If you were good to boot, you had it made. I followed that rule at every gig I ever played from then on until the end of my musical career.

One band who made a great first impression on me back then was The Beatles. I first saw them in a tiny youth club in Wednesbury, which is just outside Walsall. It wasn't even a proper rock venue, just a meeting place for kids. I

27

remember being shocked when they walked on stage. They were all wearing leathers, which was unheard of at the time, and they had their messy bowl haircuts. It was as though they had stepped straight off the street. They had picked up that look in Germany and I had never seen anything like it. Every other band on the circuit was very clean-cut and polished – they wore shiny suits and tried to look like The Shadows.

The Beatles were pretty rough and ready in those days, so they may have thought that leathers went with their sound, although the main aim was definitely to make an impact. I realised then that we had to put more effort into our appearance. You had to stand out from all the other bands. The Beatles knew that and it was obvious even then that they had something special. They weren't notably good-looking – at least I didn't think so – but they had a real stage presence. I went to that gig with a couple of mates, but they weren't as impressed as I was. I loved The Beatles' raunchy sound. They were playing a lot of Chuck Berry and R'n'B – my type of music. I never imagined for a moment that they would become as big as they did, though. Had someone told me then that I was watching what would become the biggest band in the world, I would have thought they were mad.

Fortunately, my parents didn't mind me going out to gigs all the time. I always went to venues in Walsall and Wolverhampton, so at least they knew I was nearby. A lot of the bigger bands only played Birmingham, but that was too far for me to travel. Afterwards, I would walk home. There were no buses that went directly to our estate. It was faster for me to walk than catch one bus into the centre of town, then another one home. I even walked back from Wolverhampton, which was ten miles away. It wasn't a worry in those days for kids to come home by themselves. Besides, I liked walking back from gigs. If I was with my mates, we could talk about the bands we'd seen and the best moments of the night.

*

When we began to get regular gigs, my school work started to suffer. The more bookings we got, the less I cared about classes. I was handing in assignments later and later each week, always getting a bollocking off the teachers. I started bunking off during the day too. Phil and I would attend classes in the morning, then spend entire afternoons practising at his house. We went to his because there was never anyone in during the day and it was just around the corner from school. The only class I really cared about was history. Partly, it was because I loved the subject, but it was also because we had a fantastic teacher, a bloke called Mr Dickenson. He was a real stickler, very strict and disciplined, but thanks to him the whole class passed GCE history with high marks. Of course, everyone hated his guts, but I knew he was good. He and I had a love-hate relationship. He loved me because I was well into history and I always got good marks, but he hated me for the way I looked. 'Look at the state of you, Holder,' he used to yell. I had long hair for those days, which wound him up no end.

I hadn't done much study for my GCEs, so I was shocked to find out I had passed six out of eight. I failed art and French. I was never going to pass French though. I was a disaster in the oral exams. With my accent, I couldn't pronounce any of the words properly! I was pleased that I had done well – again for my parents' sake – but I wasn't too bothered about my results. I was convinced that my future lay in music. As far as I was concerned, further education was total bollocks, at least it was for me. I still stand by that. Nothing much I learned in school was of any use to me at all in later life.

By the time I started my first year of A-levels, I was skipping school more often than I was going in. Surprisingly, my dad wasn't too bothered about it. He was even lending us the van from his window-cleaning business to go to gigs, although we still had to get someone to drive us. I think that once my dad saw us play, he realised we had talent. However, that year, to my total shock, I was made not only a prefect, but head of my house.

We had four houses, all named after admirals. Mine was Rodney. There was also Drake, Nelson and I can't remember the other. I suppose I was chosen to be head of my house because all the kids liked me and I treated even the younger ones well. I was never bossy. But it did seem odd that I was given so much responsibility, as I was constantly being told to cut my hair and I knew that not many of the teachers approved of me playing in a band. A couple of them liked the fact that I was seen as a bit of a rebel though. Maybe they thought that meant I had spirit, although what use that was in organising the football tournaments and sports days, which were my duties, I have no idea.

My final year at school coincided with The Beatles' breakthrough. It was all change for everyone my age and older after that. It's not exaggerating to say that The Beatles sparked a social revolution. Anyone who didn't live through that era could never understand just how overwhelming their influence was. People today talk about The Spice Girls selling millions of albums and becoming the biggest band in the world, but their success couldn't hold a candle to the effect that The Beatles had on people. They didn't only change the face of music, they changed the face of the '60s and the lives of an entire generation. It wasn't just The Beatles' songs that were important, it was their whole attitude. They were unlike anything that had gone before, which was why teenagers reacted so strongly to them. To us, they seemed so fresh compared to the artists who had been hogging the charts for years.

It was The Beatles who made pop mainstream in Britain. When they broke through, everyone suddenly seemed fascinated by music. It was impossible not to be. Every day, another story broke in the news about The Beatles and the mayhem they were causing wherever they went. Because I had seen them play a lot locally, it was especially exciting for me. I got a real kick out of watching them on TV. I felt like I had a bond with them, because I had been a fan before they were famous. All kids feel the same about the first bands they see. I remember staying in on Saturday nights, waiting to see The Beatles on *Thank Your Lucky Stars*. That show had replaced *Oh Boy!* as the big TV pop programme. A little later, it was *Top Of The Pops* on a Thursday evening that everyone watched. Most families stayed in specially for that. For any kid like me who dreamed of being a professional musician, it was a great opportunity to pick up tips.

As soon as The Beatles made it big, everyone tried to copy their clothes and we were no exception. It was all Cuban-heeled boots, round-neck coats and collars with a pin through them. That became the standard stage gear for every young group, regardless of the type of music they were playing. I remember being thrilled to find out where The Beatles actually bought their Cuban-heeled boots. They were from a shop in London called Anello & Davide, which still exists today. The style became mass-marketed pretty quickly, but to get an authentic pair was amazing. By then, I was earning a bit of money from the band, so I decided to buy the real thing.

It was the bassist in The Redcaps who tipped me off on where to find the boots. He worked part-time in a music shop in Walsall called Harry's and our band used to meet up there every Saturday afternoon. He had played all the big ballrooms in Birmingham on the same bill as The Beatles and had asked them where they got their gear. 'If you want the proper boots, you have to go to Drury Lane in London,' he told me. I'd been to London before, but my trip down for the boots was the first time I had walked around the city and been shopping there on my own. It was a big adventure for me.

I caught the train and took a map to help me find Drury Lane. Anello & Davide was a theatrical shoemaker that sold ballet and tap shoes. I could best describe the real Beatles boots as looking like flamenco dancers' footwear. They were short and study with very square heels. I found the shop, bought a pair and put them on straight away. I thought I was the bee's knees in them. I went into Soho on my own after that. Everyone back home had talked about the sex shops there and I wanted to take a look. I was too young to get into any of them – and too frightened to try – but I walked round peering in all the windows. Soho really was the strip capital of Britain in those days. We had no equivalent in the Midlands. I couldn't believe it when I got there. Women were just standing in doorways asking any bloke that walked by what they wanted. There were strip clubs in Birmingham, but no real red light district. It was a different world to me.

That night, I went to see my first London show. It was at The Marquee club on Wardour Street. The Who were just breaking through, but the real buzz for me was going to The Marquee. I had read all about it in the music press. It was an institution, where all the new R'n'B bands in London played. I was expecting it to be this great, glamourous venue, full of rock stars just standing around, and it turned out to be this grotty little club – but what a fantastic atmosphere!

When I was seventeen, I quit school to concentrate on music. I wasn't studying at all anymore because the band was so busy. I was coming home from gigs at 1 or 2 o'clock in the morning, then having to get up early for my first class. I was too knackered to pay any attention to the teachers. In the end, I was wagging off so much that I reckoned I might as well leave. That shocked my parents. Both of my parents had encouraged me to pursue music, but only as a hobby. The first words my dad said to me when I told him I was leaving were 'You're not'. He kept asking me what I thought I was going to do with my life. I said, 'What's the point of me staying on at school when I'm not interested anymore? Just let me give it a try. If it doesn't work out, I promise I'll go back to college.' When they saw how determined I was, they gave in, although I don't think they ever believed I could make music my profession. Until then, they hadn't even realised how seriously I was taking it.

When I told the school that I was leaving, the headmaster immediately got on to my dad. Two or three of the teachers did too. They knew my dad because he cleaned the school windows. I suppose it was assumed that I would go on to college because I had done well in my GCEs, but the truth was that I had already fallen too far behind with my work to get good A-level grades. I remember Mr Dickenson in particular being furious. He said to my dad, 'You must be mad letting your son leave school to be a musician. There's no security in that.' My dad agreed with him. It was unheard of in those days to quit education for a band. Music was thought of as a terrible occupation.

Dickenson was ex-army, so he had always got on well with my dad. They would meet up at lunchtimes and chat about the war and they were about the same age, so they had a similar outlook on life. 'Neville is wasting his life if he doesn't stay for his exams,' he told my dad. My dad was worried, but to his credit, he never tried to talk me out of leaving. 'If you want to give the band a shot, your mum and I will be behind you.'. He always told me I had talent, although I'm sure he never really thought it would work out. To this day, I respect the way he acted. He had to put up with a lot of comments from teachers about me for many years because he was still the school window-cleaner. When Slade became really successful in the early '70s, I used to send him postcards from places like Australia and Japan. He loved that because he would take them into school and just happen to mention that he had got this card from Neville from some faraway country where I was on tour. It was like a payback for all the nagging he had to endure when I left.

Watching me do well in music did genuinely make my dad happy though. I'm sure he thought that if he had been given the opportunity, he would have liked to have followed a similar path. He would have been good too. He certainly had the voice for it, and the bottle. But in his day, pursuing music must have seemed even more mad than it did for me. Today, just about every kid wants to be in a band. Back then, it was like dropping out of society.

When I left school, Phil and Pete Bickley, our bassist, quit with me. We had decided to turn professional together. By this time, Tubby had left the band and Mick Aulton stayed on at school. He's now a lecturer at Loughborough University. Phil, Pete and I found a new drummer, a great guy called Gerry Kibble. Phil's brother-in-law, Terry, had also joined us on sax and Phil was doubling up on electric organ. During our first few months out of school, we were playing a lot of local gigs in quite big venues as well as a few club dates further afield. We were earning okay money, enough to buy decent equipment, but it didn't leave us a lot to live on. There was only one option. I had to get a proper job.

To make more cash, I went to work in the office of a local firm. I was buying and selling car parts. I got the grand total of £8 for a five-day week. From the start, it was an impossible situation, worse than school. I had to be in the office by 8am every day, regardless of how late I had been out the night before. I was constantly exhausted. The boss would say, 'Noddy, you look awful. What were you up to last night?' It was obvious that my heart wasn't in it. After six months, I quit. I could see that my parents were worried. I tried to explain to them that I couldn't keep up the job and the band. They were really supportive. 'As long as you can pay your way at home, Neville, it's your life,' my dad told me. On the surface, they accepted my lifestyle, but deep down I knew they would have loved me to settle down and find a proper job. I understood their concern. They thought I was giving up any hope of financial security. I didn't see it that way. I loved my parents and I respected them, but they were never going to understand my outlook on life.

Fortunately, they didn't have long to worry about me. Shortly after I quit my sales job, the band was invited to play with a singer called Steve Brett. Back then, he was a well-known entertainer in the Midlands. He even had his own local TV show called *For Teenagers Only*, on which bands like The Beatles had performed in the early '60s. His main job was as a singer and he fronted his own group, Steve Brett and The Mavericks, who were pretty popular all over the country. 'You're going to play with Steve Brett?,' my mum said. I could tell she was impressed.

Steve approached us because his old backing band had quit to do their own thing and it was easier for him to hire a new band than put together a bunch of musicians. One night, he came backstage after a gig. 'Guys, I'm looking for new Mavericks,' he said. 'And you're my first choice.' I was pleased but not entirely surprised that Steve wanted us. The Memphis Cut-Outs had a great reputation and quite a large local following by then. The four of us had a meeting to discuss the offer, but we all knew we would eventually say yes. I had a few reservations. Steve was quite a lot older than us and he was into different music. He did a lot of Elvis, Jim Reeves, Roy Orbison and country covers, all very pop, whereas I much preferred playing R'n'B. Although his set wasn't really to our taste, we knew we had to earn a living, so we teamed up with him. 'We'll get gigs all over the country,' we told ourselves. 'We'll be famous.' We were half trying to convince ourselves that it was a good idea. At least it was a positive break. Steve was a talented performer and a good name for us to be associated with.

Joining The Mavericks gave me my first real taste of the music industry. As The Memphis Cut-Outs, we had only just begun to play outside of the Midlands. With Steve, we were going to cities such as Glasgow, Manchester and Liverpool at least once a week. We didn't actually go out on tour with Steve, but we often stayed overnight at a place if it was too long a trip home. Almost every day, we spent hours in the van driving between venues. At weekends, we sometimes did shows in two different towns on the same night. We also had several residencies, some weekly, some monthly. It was all very professional.

In the ballrooms and pubs, our usual crowd was a mix of all ages. Steve's fans tended to be well-behaved, because he had quite a clean-cut image and his material was very conventional. Wherever we played, the set was the same. For the first half of the show, we performed without Steve. I did all the singing and could choose our own songs, which included a lot of R'n'B, Motown, Little Richard and Fats Domino covers. Our job was basically to warm up the crowd before Steve appeared, so we played a good-time, party set. We always went down well, although at some gigs in the beginning it was really just Steve people wanted to watch. Halfway through the evening, he would come on and sing his more mainstream songs. For us, it was certainly an improvement on the rough pub circuit, although I never felt entirely comfortable with the musical compromise we were having to make.

By becoming The Mavericks, we suddenly found ourselves with a certain standing in the industry. We were featured in local papers a lot, usually in *The Express* and *The Star* in Wolverhampton and occasionally in the *Birmingham Mail*. We got our first piece of national press when we brought out our first single. It was released in 1965 on Columbia Records and recorded in a small studio in Birmingham. Naturally, I was thrilled about beginning my recording career, even though I was only playing guitar and doing backing vocals. In truth, it was a pretty uneventful experience. I had no idea what to expect. None of us had ever been in a studio before. We went in for half a day and recorded three or four tracks. One, a Buddy Holly cover called 'Wishing', became the A-side of the single. All the songs were from our live set and we played exactly as we did every night on stage. The only difference was that there were mics set up between the amps. That was how everyone recorded in those days. There were no fancy studio techniques to change your sound. You just went in, played for a couple of hours, then left. It was very un-rock'n'roll.

Over the next couple of months, we released a total of three singles on Columbia. They were all recorded in the same studio in Birmingham and all were songs lifted from our live set, plus a couple of B-sides that Steve had written himself. The second one was called 'Sad, Lonely and Blue' and the third was a cover of 'Chains of My Heart', both very country. Now all three are collector's items, but when they came out, they didn't make much of a splash. They did alright locally, but none were big hits, certainly not on a national scale. I wasn't too bothered by their lack of commercial success. I was just excited to have our own record in the shops. I'm sure Steve was disappointed, because the songs were pretty good. They had the potential to be hits – although they were probably a bit too old-fashioned to do really well – but they were never pushed by the record company except in the Midlands. I guess we didn't have a big enough following in other parts of the country to justify much promotional expense.

Our only other recording with Steve took place a few months later in London. We were to be produced by Joe Meek, which was a very big deal in those days. Joe was always referred to in the press as The Legendary Joe Meek. He was probably Britain's first independent pop producer. He was behind big hits such as The Honeycombs' 'Have I The Right' and he had just had a monster smash all over the world with 'Telstar' by the Tornados. It was at No.1 in Britain for five weeks and it was the first English rock'n'roll record ever to top the American charts. When the BBC showed Neil Armstrong landing on the moon, 'Telstar' was the song they used as a soundtrack.

Steve knew someone who knew Joe Meek and had arranged for us to work with him. I thought it was amazing that we were off to London to record with this supposedly mastermind producer who we had heard so much about. When we got there, it was all a bit of a let down. Joe was famous for his bizarre recording techniques. Basically, he had set a studio up in his bathroom for the echo effects and that was where he made all his hits. We had imagined that this notorious bathroom would be filled with state-of-the-art equipment and that his house would be like a palace. In fact, he lived in a rented flat above a shop with just one shoddy little bathroom where all the amps were set up. Artists had to piss as well as play in there. We couldn't believe our eyes. He was this big name and he worked in a dump.

I don't remember much about Joe except that he was a portly bloke, much older than us, with slicked-back hair. I don't think he said two words to anyone except Steve the whole time we were there. I couldn't even say what songs we recorded with him, but none of them was ever released. That didn't surprise me. Even at the time, I thought what we were doing was a pile of shite. I remember thinking, 'How on earth has this guy ever produced a hit record in this place?'

For the recording, we all stood out on the landing, playing our instruments, while Joe was in his control box, mixing. It was like a scene from *Spinal Tap*. It was obvious even to us that Joe was a total loony. Truly, he was mad. In the end, he committed suicide. He shot his landlady, then turned the gun on himself. Our experience with Joe had a profound effect on me. It was the first time I had met someone famous and not understood the appeal. I had thought of him as a star purely because I was reading about him in the *NME* every week. Suddenly, I realised that having a load of hits to his name didn't make him a god. He was no better than us and we were just a bunch of hicks from Wolverhampton.

Whatever my reservations about Steve Brett, it was while playing with him that I got my first taste of a real rock'n'roll lifestyle. Thanks to our live reputation, we were offered our first job abroad. It was for eight weeks in Germany, playing two consecutive month-long residencies at clubs in Frankfurt and Cologne. At the time, British musicians were hugely popular in Germany, largely because all the Liverpool bands had spent so much time there before they became famous. It was The Beatles who had started the trend. Their career had basically kicked off at The Star Club in Hamburg, after which every city in Germany wanted to bring over English acts because their local groups were still playing traditional oompah music, not new rock'n'roll. By the time we arrived in Frankfurt, some bands had taken to touring there non-stop because the money was so good. In our first week, we took over from a band which included Noel Redding, who went on to be Jimi Hendrix's bassist.

We were totally unprepared for the lifestyle of bands abroad. I don't think even Steve had been to Germany before, so none of us knew what to expect. Our first four weeks were spent at a club in Frankfurt called The Storyville, which was one of a chain of German venues owned by the same bloke. It was not far from several American Air Force bases, so a lot of our audience came from there. We played two different sets every night. From 9pm until about midnight, the crowd was made up mostly of Germans. We would perform all our poppier songs for them. Then there was a curfew, when the younger locals had to go home. From midnight until 2 or 3am, the Americans came in. They loved both Steve Brett's country songs and our soul stuff, although with the black Americans, we were probably even more popular than Steve. They were very long gigs for us. Every night, we played either five or six sets of forty-five minutes, between each of which we had a fifteen-minute break. That was Monday to Friday. At the weekend, we had to start at 2 o'clock on a Saturday afternoon and work through to 4am. Then we began again at 4pm Sunday afternoon and finished at 2am.

During our sets, we played a lot of requests. Whenever I sang a soul song which one of the Americans had asked for, they would buy us bottles of beer and Cognac chasers as a thank you. We could only drink in the fifteen-minute breaks, so whenever we came off stage, there would be a table full of free drinks just waiting for us. Often, we had to knock back six or seven beers and brandy chasers in a row. If you didn't finish them during that break, the waiters would clear them away or drink them themselves. You can imagine the worsening state I was in as the gig went on. After two or three breaks, I'd be smashed. Usually, the last set was instrumentals. By then, I was too out of my tree to sing and play at the same time. We'd have to resort to jamming Booker T and The MGs' 'Green Onions' for 45 minutes.

Musically, every band that went to Germany improved ten-fold. Partly, it was because the shows were so long. We already had quite a wide repertoire, but we still had to add dozens of new songs to our set every week. Those gigs were also a great lesson in learning very quickly how to really entertain an audience. You couldn't go on, stand there and just slum it all night. The Germans expected a proper show. The madder you were, the better their reaction. That's when I started developing ideas for performances which would involve the crowd. After a couple of weeks, it had become our gimmick. The audience waited to see who we would choose and what we would do. We also started to get a bit eccentric with our clothes. A few times, we even ended up performing in dresses just for effect. Back then, the standard R'n'B gear was jeans and a leather waistcoat, which was a look the Germans loved because seeing English bands wearing leather reminded them of The Beatles. When you had the same people coming to see you several times a week though, you had to be a bit more adventurous.

Frankfurt was the first time any of us had played outside the UK. I had never even been abroad until then. Apart from Steve, we were all only eighteen or nineteen. The whole trip was a real eye-opener. It was a totally different way of life from the one we had back home, even though we were basically doing the same job. In Walsall, I was still living with my mum and dad, as were the other lads. In Frankfurt, the six us were sharing a flat in the centre of town. It was where all the visiting bands stayed. One lot would move in for a month, then move out on the day that the next lot arrived. The combination of our new-found independence and the rock'n'roll lifestyle was lethal. It was debauchery from start to finish. We just drank, played and shagged as much as we wanted, with a few pills to keep our energy levels up. Then we spent our days sleeping or trying to recover from the night before. I had never been a serious drinker until then and I'm sure that's what started me off. I was out of my head every night. Plus, the German women were all over us. They loved English bands. I think all of us pulled on the first night. The extra-curricular activities of the music business back home was a teddy bear's picnic compared to what went on in Germany. Thank God!

Although you had to work hard for it, the money in Germany was always good. In Frankfurt, each band member was earning £25 a week. Steve was on more because he was the big name, but we didn't mind. £25 was a lot of dough in those days. I had been getting £8 for a full-time office job back in Walsall, so I was happy. The only problem was that we were all spending more than we made. We pissed it up the wall or wasted it on women or gambling. After a couple of weeks, a guy who worked at the club noticed our predicament and offered us a way of making some extra cash. He was into all sorts of unusual pastimes. I was only ever involved in one of them and it was only once – honestly – when I was totally skint. What he liked to do was lie in the bath, under a glass sheet, and get young lads like us to shit on him. 'I'll pay you a whole week's wages if you'll do it,' he told us. So I did. It wasn't an enjoyable experience by any means, but I was broke and starving. Besides, it could have been a lot worse. I think I just convinced myself that I had to crap somewhere and got on with it.

YOU

GUYS

PROJECT!

3

When I got back to England after our time abroad, I quit Steve Brett's band. It wasn't working out as well as I had hoped and I was bored of supporting someone else. I wanted to be the frontman. Steve and I had been having a few arguments about money and had fallen out quite badly before we left Germany. The wages we were getting over there were good, but in Britain he was keeping most of our fee because of his name. I didn't think it was fair because, by then, the band was being rebooked as much on the strength of me as it was on him. Plus, Steve no longer had his TV show. He may not have realised it, but he wasn't the TV star he used to be.

When I told Steve I was quitting, he was a bit surprised, but I think he knew our relationship had come to an end. He had left us in Germany with all the equipment and no money and had caught the train back himself. We had had to wire our parents for some cash so that we could get home. Steve knew I wouldn't put up with stuff like that anymore. I thought Phil would leave The Mavericks with me, but he didn't. He wanted to stay because that way he could be sure of a regular income. The bassist and the drummer did quit though. The original plan was for the three of us to find another guitarist and regroup under a new name. The others were keen to start auditioning straight away, but I wanted to wait. I thought we should decide what type of music we wanted to make before we began doing gigs again. I wanted a change, but I didn't know what it would be. I did know that I was desperate to get away from the Elvis and country stuff we had been doing with Steve and into more soul music, like James Brown. But that wasn't enough. We had to hit on something that would make us special.

A few weeks later, while I was still between bands, I bumped into Dave Hill and Don Powell in the street in Wolverhampton. They were two local musicians who I had known for a few years from the Midlands circuit. We had met a couple of times when I was with The Memphis Cut-Outs, but we had got talking after playing on the same bills when I was with Steve Brett. Both Don and Dave were the same age as me. We were all eighteen. They hadn't gone to the same school, but they had grown up not far from each other on the outskirts of Wolverhampton, which was only five or six miles from where I lived in Walsall. Their background was exactly the same as mine too, very working-class.

Both Dave and Don were in a local band called the 'N Betweens. Dave was the guitarist and Don was the drummer. Don had formed the band years before when he was still at school and Dave had joined a little later from another group after the original guitarist left. The 'N Betweens were basically a blues band. They were very popular in the Midlands. They had been playing the same circuit to the same size audiences that I had with with Steve Brett. Their recording career was pretty similar too. They had put out a few singles on a French label called Barclay, but they hadn't had any hits outside of the Midlands.

The last time I had seen Dave and Don was on the way over to Germany. We had met totally by chance on the ferry. They were booked to do a stint in Dortmund when we were in Frankfurt. The three of us went for a few drinks in the bar and Dave had told me that they were going to split up their band as soon as they got back to Britain. He said they wanted to take their music in a different direction and that they were bored of playing just blues. He asked me then if I was interested in being their new singer. I was shocked, but also flattered. I said thanks for the offer but explained that I was quite happy with my own situation, which I was at the time.

When I bumped into Dave and Don in the street in Wolverhampton, I told them I had left Steve Brett, which they hadn't heard. Immediately, Dave asked if I would reconsider his offer to join them. Part of me wanted to say yes straight away. Another part of me nearly said no. I liked Don a lot, but I had never been sure about Dave. The first time I had properly met the pair of them was at the Kingfisher Country Club, which was quite a posh venue just outside Wolverhampton. Both Steve Brett and the 'N Betweens were on the same bill that night. Don and I had hit it off immediately, but Dave had been a bit aloof. He came up and said, 'Hi,' then more or less ignored me for the rest of the evening. I was a bit put out until I realised that he was like that with everyone. Dave – or H as we always called him – was never one of the lads and he never wanted to be. Even years later, rather than hang out with the rest of the band, he preferred to strut with the ladies. A lot of blokes didn't like him for that. They thought he was a real show-off and self-obsessed. Underneath – as I later found out – Dave wasn't like that at all, but that was always his public persona.

Don was a different kettle of fish altogether. On the outside, he was very quiet and shy, almost timid. When you got to know him though, he was very very funny. He was one of those people who constantly came out with brilliant one-liners. On stage, he looked like this mad tearaway drummer, but that wasn't the real Don. He was so unassuming. I never once heard Don raise his voice or have an argument. I liked him straight away.

I eventually agreed to go for one rehearsal. Dave and Don hadn't officially split up the old 'N Betweens, but they had already recruited Jimmy Lea to play bass. He was still at school. They also had a singer, Johnny Howles, who had been with them for a while and who they intended to keep on. It turned out that they only wanted me as a second singer and an additional guitarist. When they told me that,

I almost backed out. Sharing the vocals would put me in the same position I had been in with Steve Brett. In the end, I went anyway. I wasn't doing anything else at the time and I liked the 'N Betweens. I was pleased that Dave and Don were interested in experimenting with their music, rather than just copying the hit acts of the day. I also discovered that they were planning to get rid of Johnny, the other singer, after six months. They liked him, but they told me that he was lazy and he hated to rehearse. The other problem was that although Johnny was an excellent blues singer and harmonica player, he couldn't do any other type of music. Unfortunately, he was the one member of the original line-up that they couldn't sack. They had six months of gigs already booked and promoters were expecting to see a familiar face up front.

Our first rehearsal took place at The Three Men In A Boat, the pub just across the road from my house. I had played there a lot with The Memphis Cut-Outs when I was still at school. We had to meet under cover so that the other 'N Betweens wouldn't find out. The secrecy made it seem quite exciting. We chose The Three Men In A Boat as a venue because it was outside Wolverhampton. If we had gone to the 'N Betweens' regular rehearsal hall, the others would have been sure to hear about it. They knew it was on the cards that Dave and Don were splitting the band, but they didn't realise they had hired new musicians. I think Dave and Don wanted to keep it quiet because they didn't know if Jimmy and I were going to work out. They may have asked us to join, but there was still the chance that we would sound terrible together.

That afternoon, we rehearsed three or four numbers that we all knew. I think we did some James Brown and Chuck Berry covers. The four of us clicked straight away. We knew right then that we had something special. All that was left was for Dave and Don to tell the other 'N Betweens. I didn't have anyone to tell because I wasn't in a band. Neither did Jimmy. He was still at school. I remember his mum and dad trying to talk him out of leaving to join the band. He had been offered a place at art college and they wanted him to finish school and go on there, but there was no way he was staying. He knew that the 'N Betweens were a well-rated local band and he was already a big fan. Jimmy wasn't so keen on me though. We had never met before the rehearsal, but he had seen me play with The Memphis Cut-Outs and Steve Brett and he knew what type of music I was into. He loved the bluesy sound of the old 'N Betweens and had hoped the new line-up would be playing more or less the same songs. I could tell he was disappointed when Dave and Don introduced me as the second singer, rather than just a guitarist. It was obvious that he preferred Johnny, although he didn't have the nerve to say so.

The first thing we did as a band was go shopping. We needed a new look. We didn't want people to think we were just an updated 'N Betweens. We had to be fresh and original. Until then, the band had worn the traditional blues uniform of waistcoats and checked shirts. We ditched those and went into Birmingham to buy something more striking. Dave said, 'Let's all get gear that no one else would wear.' I was up for that. It was shock tactics. Jimmy had never been in a proper band before and when he saw what Dave and I were buying, he was flabbergasted. 'You're not really going to wear those outfits on stage,' he kept saying. He thought we were joking. We were going through racks of the most garish over-the-top clothes we could find, egging each other on. The stuff we were choosing was all very colourful, not unlike what we would later wear in the glam days, although it wasn't glittery. I picked out a long tartan jacket and Dave found a purple velvet coat with a stuck-up collar. The pair of us were determined to be different. No one was going for outrageous outfits, so we adopted them.

Our new image was perfect for Dave. He loved to be centre of attention and he had no shame about how he looked. Jokes about his clothes were like water off a duck's back to him. He used to pose around Wolverhampton in a cloak, looking like a Shakespearian actor. He was also mad keen on very high Cuban-heeled boots. Dave had a real hang-up about his height. He was only five foot two. The first time I met him, I couldn't get over how odd he looked when he walked. He sort of tip-toed around in these heels. I never saw him without them. Another of Dave's obsessions was his hair. Most blokes in bands had long hair, but Dave's was always much longer than everyone else's. It was poker straight and he already had that short fringe cut into it. His hair was his trademark.

The others were never as outrageous as me and Dave. Lookswise, that shopping trip pretty much summed us all up. Dave was in a league of his own, but I wasn't far behind him. Next came Don. He quite liked dressing up, but he knew his limits. Then there was Jim and Johnny. They weren't into it at all. At least Jim was prepared to make an effort. He bought some quite colourful stuff just to fit in with the rest of us, but Johnny was having none of it. He insisted on wearing a dark suit whenever he was on stage.

We played our first gig as the new 'N Betweens on 1 April 1966. It was at Walsall Town Hall. I was relieved that it was in my local area because, I knew I could count on my friends for support. We were dreading getting stick from fans of the original band. Some of them were not at all pleased that Dave and Don had changed the line-up. There was a lot of bad feeling about it. We could feel the uneasiness in the audience even before we went on stage. It was horrible. I had visions of us being booed off or of me being pelted with pint glasses. As it turned out, we needn't have worried. There were a few scary moments at the start of the set, but ten minutes in, the animosity had gone and everyone was getting into it. We had rehearsed for weeks to make sure we were good and we won over even the die-hard old fans. Our new look helped a lot. Most people were so stunned when we walked on stage that they didn't know how to react. By the time they got their heads round our outfits, they knew that they liked the music. We were delighted. We had jumped the first hurdle and we were still standing.

For the next few months, most of our shows were in the Wolverhampton area. We had several residencies once a week or once a month at various local venues. We played the George Hotel in Walsall on Monday nights and Aldridge Community Centre on Sundays. Our other regular gigs were at the Parkhall and Connaught hotels and the Ship and Rainbow pub, all in Wolverhampton. Residencies were our bread and butter work. Whatever other gigs we got, we looked on as a bonus.

Every night, Johnny and I would split the set fifty/fifty. I came on first and did stuff like Lee Dorsey's 'Working in the Coalmine' and some Tamla Motown. Then Johnny would take over and do more blues-based material. Even though we only did covers, we always came up with our own versions of them. We had decided by then that we liked being a loud band. It's hard to describe what we sounded like, but we were basically turning Temptations and Four Tops hits into noisy guitar tunes.

On Sundays, we used to put on a special show called *The Sunday Service*. I would come on stage dressed as a vicar and tell dirty gags between the songs. It was an act we became well-known for. A lot of bands did bits and pieces of comedy or impersonations on stage – like a cabaret – but we steered clear of that. We wanted to be different. Besides, it wouldn't have suited our set. We were pretty raucous even then. Dirty gags were great because they got the audience involved. That was important to me. I always encouraged audience participation. I'd often pull punters up on stage to sing songs like Wilson Pickett's 'Land of 1000 Dances' with us. Sometimes, I'd just pick on one person and make them a part of the show. There was a bloke at the Ship and Rainbow who would get on stage with us and sing 'Skippy the Bush Kangaroo'. Everyone knew him. You could feel the whole crowd waiting for him to do his piece. A few of the stunts were preplanned like that, but mostly they just happened. They almost always went down a storm. There were a few audiences that didn't like that sort of thing though. If they preferred the cabaret-type acts, our show would go down like a lead balloon and we wouldn't be rebooked.

Our first big gig was opening for Cream at Wolverhampton Civic Hall. That was such a buzz. They were a mad bunch. Their drummer, Ginger Baker, always blew me away. For a start, he had a double drum kit. I mean, no one had two drum kits. He loved showing off. At one gig we played with them, there was only one tiny dressing room at the side of the stage. All of us and all of Cream were crammed into it. Suddenly, Ginger decided to set his two drum kits up in the middle of everyone. Then he started dancing on top of them. He was totally out of his tree. I thought it was great. I thought we had hit the big time, rubbing shoulders with all these eccentric rock'n'rollers.

After Cream, we supported dozens of big bands, like John Mayall's Blues Breakers and The Move, which was Roy Wood's group. We had known The Move for years because they were from the same area as us. They would soon be having hits, but at that time they were still part of the local scene. The Midlands was full of great musicians. Two who I was quite pally with were John Bonham and Robert Plant. I even roadied for Robert a few times when I didn't have any gigs of my own. At the time, he was in a band called Listen with two of my old school mates. We also worked with The Idle Race, which was Jeff Lynne's group before he went on to form Electric Light Orchestra with Roy Wood. It was a really exciting time. I was surrounded by brilliant musicians, who everyone knew were destined for fame.

Although our band was doing fairly well and we were making a bit of money, we had one big problem – Johnny. Relations between him and Dave and Don had been going downhill since the start. As it turned out, they were right about him being lazy. It didn't bother me too much because I hadn't been with him for long, but Dave and Don were sick and tired of him not turning up for rehearsals. By the time we got near the end of our first six months, the three of them weren't getting on at all. Johnny didn't care that he was pissing Dave and Don off. He knew he would be booted out of the band after the booked gigs were over. His best pal had already been sacked, so he wasn't that keen to stay anyway.

Matters came to a head just after we'd played a week in Torquay. We were then due to do four nights at The Blue Lagoon ballroom in Newquay, then one show in Plymouth. The Torquay dates had gone really well and we were all having a laugh. I even thought Dave and Don might have patched things up with Johnny. We didn't realise until later, but our opening act in Newquay had Roger Taylor, in his pre-Queen days, as their drummer.

We stayed for a week in a caravan in Newquay and had to drive from there to the gig in Plymouth. That afternoon, we could tell that Johnny was in a weird mood. As we were about to set off for Plymouth, he said, 'I can't make it to the gig tonight.' It came totally out of the blue. I can't remember what his excuse was, but he had probably pulled a bird and wanted to stay in Newquay. Either that or he was just trying to be difficult. He thought we would be furious when he said he wasn't coming. In fact, we were rubbing our hands with glee. What Johnny didn't know was that we were waiting for a chance to play without him. We wanted to find out how we would cope when he left.

Plymouth was our first ever gig as a four-piece. I was fairly confident we could carry it off, but I don't think Dave and Don were so sure. As it turned out, Johnny was barely missed. We went down brilliantly. Afterwards, we drove back to Newquay. We were buzzing because the gig had been such a success. When we got to the caravan, Johnny was lying in bed. He had finished whatever he had been doing and was pretending to be asleep. We had brought some girls and a load of booze back with us, so we just partied around him. A week later, he was gone.

For the next month or so, Dave and Don searched for a replacement for Johnny. They had wanted him out of the group, but they still thought that we needed two singers.

Fortunately for me, there weren't many good singers around at the time who would have suited our style of music. I remember that Robert Plant was one of the names mentioned. The others didn't know him, but I did. I don't know if anyone ever actually approached Robert, but certainly he was one of only two or three names in the frame. Personally, I didn't mind if we got another singer or not. I knew that I could front the band by myself and I preferred being in a four-piece. Dave and Don weren't convinced though. They felt more comfortable as a five-piece, because that's what they had been used to.

In the end, it was our roadie, a guy called Graham Swinerton – or Swin as we called him – who convinced Dave and Don that we should stick with one singer. He had been one of Don's best mates since school and he later became our tour manager. 'You guys are mad to get another singer,' he told Dave and Don. 'Noddy can do the job fine.' The pair of them agreed to try me out as sole frontman for six months. They didn't have much choice. We hadn't found anyone to replace Johnny and it was obvious that the likes of Robert Plant weren't going to join us. It wasn't that their bands were better, it was just that most singers liked to be in charge. We were very much a democracy. No one person was going to have the final say with us.

My six-month trial period never really happened. After our first few gigs as a four-piece, we forgot all about it. We didn't just go down well, we went down better than ever. We were still called the 'N Betweens, but that was really the start of Slade.

When I wasn't playing or rehearsing, I went to as many gigs as I could. It was good to know what our contemporaries were up to. I remember seeing the Spencer Davis Group for the first time. They played at a ballroom in West Bromwich. The original 'N Betweens had supported them several times and Dave and Don had told me all about them. Like everyone else in the Midlands, they had raved about this amazing kid singer called Stevie Winwood.

I was dying to see the band for myself, but when they walked on stage, I was really disappointed. Apart from the fact that Stevie was only fifteen, there seemed to be nothing remarkable about them. They didn't even attempt to make a big entrance; they just strolled on. They also had the smallest amps I'd ever seen. They started to play an old blues number, very quietly, just repeating the intro over and over. It seemed to go on for ages. Both Spencer and Stevie's brother, Muff, were singing, but they were barely audible. I was totally puzzled. 'What is it about this band that everyone loves?' I asked someone. I couldn't understand the appeal. Then all of a sudden, Stevie broke in with the first verse of the song. His voice was incredible, really gruff. He was just a little kid but he sounded exactly like Ray Charles. It was fantastic. The Spencer Davis Group already had a great reputation in all the R'n'B clubs. Everyone said they were about to break big and I could understand why.

Another group I loved at that time were Denny Laine's Moody Blues. I had played with them when I was in The Memphis Cut-Outs, well before they had their first hit with 'Go Now'. They were now one of the happening acts. I saw how much they had improved and I knew that we had to do the same if we were to break through too. Don and I often went together to watch our favourite bands and suss out why they were good. We paid attention to the songs they were playing, but it wasn't really the music we wanted to copy. Having seen The Beatles early on in their career, I knew that they hadn't changed much musically by the time they made it. They may have had more confidence, but that was something we certainly weren't lacking in. We never asked any bands for advice though. We were far too proud. We preferred to study from the audience.

One of the biggest lessons we learnt from watching other bands was the importance of good equipment. We still had pretty basic gear, but we could tell how much better we would be if we had more money to spend. We would also be able to play louder. Not that we had ever been quiet. We had gone flat out on volume from the start, regardless of the size of venue we were playing. Promoters were always moaning at us to turn the sound down, but the audience loved it. Our aim was to hit people right between the eyes from the start of our set. The same thinking was behind our garish stage gear – the shock factor. We weren't interested in building up the show. We went in all guns blazing from the off. We wanted to pin people against the wall within a minute, then try to take them further still. We were good at it too.

We soon realised that the strength of our sound had become our trademark. Musically, it was what set us apart from our contemporaries. We decided to play that up. That was when we hit on a brilliant trick. Today, every band has a PA system, through which the sound comes out all over the stage. Back then, even the big acts had only a tiny PA for the vocals and a backline of amplifiers. The problem was that you had separate amps for the lead guitar, rhythm guitar and bass and that was exactly how the crowd heard it. If you were standing in front of the bassist, for example, you heard him a lot louder than anyone else. Then Swin and I came up with the idea of rewiring our amps so that they all linked up. I can hardly believe no one had thought of it before. The result was that Dave, Jim and I came out of speakers on both sides of the stage. It was like a rudimentary monitor system. Wherever you stood in the crowd, you could hear the whole band. It sounds simple, but no one else was doing it.

Our new trick marked a turning point for us. Dave and Don had been searching for a new sound since the day I joined and as soon as we started messing around with the amps, we knew exactly what it was going to be. It was Dave who had suggested we have three lead guitarists. In other bands, guitarists played lead, rhythm or bass. Although Jim did actually play bass, he played it like a lead guitar. Even with Motown riffs we would all play lead, but with different harmonies. Together with our sneaky wiring, the effect was fantastic. We had a wall of sound behind us that other bands couldn't believe. Even the big-name bands we supported were shocked that we could get this incredibly loud noise out of such small amps. I can still picture the likes of The Tremeloes, The Hollies and Marmalade all asking us how we did it. We just said we turned everything up to ten. It was a mass of wires backstage, so there was no way anyone was going to guess. I suppose they thought we had found some flash way to boost the amps. It wasn't a technique we perfected overnight though. We developed it over several years. When we finally got it right, it freaked audiences out. They loved it because it was a totally new sound. It was the sound that would later make us famous.

I had been with the 'N Betweens barely a year when we were given the chance to cut our first record. The old band had put out a couple of singles, but they were just basic blues tracks straight from their live set. This new record was a much bigger deal because it was to be produced by Kim Fowley, who was a famous pop Svengali from the States. Kim was like an LA equivalent of Joe Meek. He had produced hits for loads of American groups. British audiences knew him best for a song called 'Nut Rocker' by B. Bumble and The Stingers. It was a boogie-woogie instrumental based on Tchaikovsky's *Nutcracker Suite* and had been a UK No.1 a few years earlier. He had also produced *Alley Oop* by the Hollwood Argyles. Like Meek, Kim was a bit mad, although in a much more endearing way. He was also well-known for recording in bathrooms, which did worry me a little.

We met Kim Fowley completely by accident. We were playing a show in a basement club called Tiles in Oxford Street in London. We rarely played London, so we weren't top of the bill. Halfway through our set, we noticed this incredibly tall, streaky figure in the middle of the crowd. It was hard to miss him. Not only was he wearing a cowboy hat, which made him stick out head and shoulders above everyone else, but he was doing this freaky dancing. When we came off stage, he appeared in our dressing room. He just strolled through the door. 'I'm going to make you guys stars,' he said. That was his opening line. He had a really strong American accent and he played it up to the full. The four of us looked up at this weirdo in his hat and hippy clothes and wondered who the hell he was. At first, we just thought he was a mad fan. Then he told us his name. We knew him immediately from his records. We were astonished. Kim Fowley was not only in our dressing room, but he was going to make us famous!

Kim was based in LA at a label called Rendezvous Records, but he was in London looking for bands. One band in particular. He was after a bunch of musicians who he could take back to the States and pass off as Them, Van Morrison's old band. They had recently had a big hit in America with 'Gloria'. Before they had completed their tour, they had split up. Kim's idea was to find a replacement group who he could put out on the road as Them and cash in on their success. That happened a lot in the '60s. It still happens today with bands from that era. I'm sure there's a Mamas and The Papas still touring Germany that has nothing to do with the original group. At one time in Britain in the '60s there were nine different Drifters on the road. Naturally, audiences minded when they turned up to the gigs, but they didn't realise they weren't getting the real thing until after the set had started and by then they had paid to get in.

Kim loved our band from the second he saw us. We were a revelation to him. We didn't sound like anyone he had ever heard before, either in America or England. He had also never seen a singer like me who encouraged so much audience participation. I was always chatting to the crowd and getting people up on stage. Kim decided that we were his favourite British band and wanted to turn us into Them. It didn't matter that Van Morrison's lot were from Belfast and that we were from the Midlands. When we refused, Kim kept offering us more money. Eventually, we told him we weren't going to change our minds and that he should look for another act. We thought then that he would walk out the door and we would never hear from him again. Instead, he insisted on us staying down in London so that we could record together.

The next day, Kim took us round to lots of record companies. We were all excited because we thought we had got our first foot in the door. Just being around Kim was a surreal experience. For a start, he was a tall beanpole freak from LA and we had never met anyone like that before. He dressed in long flowing clothes and he always wore his cowboy hat. No one looked like that in the Midlands. He was a real hippy, completely out to lunch. At least, that was how he appeared. Kim was also the first person ever to tell us that we were going to be stars. He saw something in us, even in those early days, and that gave us a lot of confidence. His favourite saying to us was 'you guys project'. He said it every time he saw us.

The first place Kim took us that day was to the bank, because he had to get some cash. He had us all trailing in a line behind him. God knows why we were doing it. It was just Kim; he had this aura. When he got to the woman at the counter, instead of asking for his money, he said, 'Take a good look at these boys behind me. They're going to be one of the biggest bands in the world one day. You mark my words, lady. I've never been so sure about anything in my life.' We just stood there, shuffling our feet and looking awkward. Kim gave everyone the same line, wherever we went. That's why he was so successful. He had the gift of the gab. Basically, he was a blagger. He could walk straight into all the big record companies and demand to be seen. If someone didn't know him, they had always heard of him. His reputation preceded him.

We returned home, but a few days later we came back down to London and Kim took us to a little studio in Denmark Street called Regent Sound. I don't think we even had a whole day in there, just an afternoon, but we cut four tracks. It was mainly songs we had been doing on stage, including one called 'You Better Run' which was originally by The Young Rascals. A lot of the material in our set wasn't well-known in Britain. 'You Better Run' had been a No.1 in America, but I don't think it was even released over here. We sought out songs like that on purpose. We used to go to a record shop in Birmingham called The Diskery for all the new American imports. We spent most Saturday afternoons there browsing through the racks and asking the guys behind the counter what had just come in. 'You Better Run' was a record from there. We loved it and we were already playing quite a few other Young Rascals songs in our set.

Kim obviously knew 'You Better Run', but he had never heard anyone play it like we did. We recorded our version with him for the A-side of the single, plus a couple of other covers. We also recorded a song called 'Evil Witchman', which Kim made up on the spot in the studio. I was playing this riff and he started scribbling down some daft words and that was it. It was done in two takes and it became the B-side. Kim got a deal for it to be released on EMI. That was our first proper single. It actually went to No.1 in local charts in the Midlands, because we had a name there and our fans knew the song from our live shows. I guess we had hoped that single might make us famous, but we weren't really sure what would happen. We were very green and we had no idea how you could tell if you were about to become a star. We were pretty pleased just to release a record. We thought it was great to have a single out on a major label after such a short time together. More than anything, it was a big confidence boost to know that someone like Kim Fowley saw potential in us. Even though he was a nutter, he was well-respected in the business. He was shrewd and he could spot a hit. He didn't back any old band either. He had to really rate you to produce your record and we knew he loved us.

We rarely saw Kim again after our day in the studio. He was back in the States before the single even came out. He had never intended to stay in England for more than a couple of weeks and our band certainly weren't going to keep him here. We were a one-off for him, a little labour of love. The west coast of America was his home and he wanted to get back to all his big acts there. He remained a huge fan of ours though. Later, when we became Slade, Kim would turn up to our LA gigs. In the '70s, he put together an all-girl group called The Runaways and got them to record 'Mama Weer All Crazee Now'. That was his favourite Slade song. One of the last times I saw Kim was in the early '80s, when we were on tour in Germany. We were in an hotel, waiting for the lift. When the doors opened, there was Kim. He was exactly the same, still long and stringy, but he had a suit on and he looked very dapper. The first words out of his mouth were, 'Didn't I say you guys would be stars. I told you, didn't I? I always said you could project.' He remembered it all perfectly. He had an amazing mind. He was a freak, but a smart freak.

Our deal with EMI was hinged on Kim's involvement, so when he went, the label more or less lost interest. They didn't know anything about us and we weren't considered a long-term project. They did push the single a bit and they set us up for a few press interviews. They were waiting to see if the song took off on a national scale. When it didn't, they made one last attempt to get us a hit. We were taken to cut a couple of tracks at Abbey Road. As soon as we got to the studio, we knew that The Beatles were recording there, because their cars were outside. All four of them used to drive around London in black minis with dark tinted windows. We didn't see them when we were there, but we could hear all these weird sounds coming out of the control room next door. They were locked away in another studio recording *Sgt. Pepper*. We couldn't make out any songs, but they were obviously having one of those days when they were just trying out loads of tricks, like running tapes backwards. It sounded bizarre to us, because no one had experimented that way with music before. We were thrilled to be in the same studio as The Beatles. The tracks we did there never came to anything, but it was worth it for the buzz. The Beatles were Gods to every band and we had recorded next door to them.

HALFWAY

TO

PARADISE

4

My first trip abroad with the 'N Betweens was to Germany. By then, quite a few Wolverhampton bands were working out there. We were keen to go because we knew it would be good training. Groups always improved when they went to Germany because the hours were so long. We were booked to do a month at a club called The Star Palace in Kiel, which is a coastal town north of Hamburg. Lots of English bands had played there. We drove over in our van via the ferry to Holland, which was a hell of a long haul. When we arrived at the venue, we were shocked. We had expected it to be a typical dingy club. Instead, it was a big old converted cinema with a raised stage, a dancefloor and an area full of tables and chairs. It was a proper gig. It was also a real heavy place. Being in a coastal town, it attracted a lot of sailors, which in those days meant trouble. We knew what sort of establishment it was as soon as we saw the waiters. Jim was the first to notice what they were wearing. 'Oh my God,' he said, as soon as we walked in the place. 'They're all carrying guns!'

Until we turned up, the club's resident band had been Paul Raven and The Boston Showband. They were a well-known act in Germany and The Star Palace was one of their regular gigs. We were one of two groups who had been brought in to replace them while they took a month off. Years later, Paul Raven, their frontman, became Gary Glitter. That was our first encounter with him. He was probably in his twenties, but he looked pretty much as he does now, a rocker in lots of leather gear with an Elvis-style quiff. The Germans loved that look. In the '60s, there were a lot of Irish showbands on tour. They were groups with a vast line-up of musicians, including a brass section. They were popular because they could play all sorts of music, from Irish jigs to rock'n'roll. At the time, Gary – or Paul Raven – was doing mainly rock'n'roll and R'n'B covers.

At The Star Palace, two bands performed every night. Each took it in turn to play three hour-long sets. Both also stayed in the venue. Most clubs put acts up at a nearby flat, but this place was so big that it had a dormitory downstairs with bunk beds. The Boston Showband were on a month's break, but they were still staying at the venue. They were already installed in the main dorm. The group that we were playing with had taken the second smaller dorm before we arrived. There were no beds left for us, so we had to sleep on the stairs in little camp beds. We were skint when we got there. We had spent all our money on petrol for the van and our ferry fare over and German promoters were notorious for being tight. They would never give you any of your fee upfront.

Fortunately, Gary realised our predicament. 'I'll take you around town and show you all the cheapest places to eat,' he offered. I remember him taking us to this local cafe. All we could afford was pea and ham soup, so we ate it non-stop. The lot of us were farting for a week. When we were given a bit of money, we switched to eating omelettes. Most of our first pay packet was spent on booze in the club. We basically lived there. We worked from 8pm to 4am, playing alternate hours with the other band. If we went out to a bar after we finished, we wouldn't get to bed until 7am. Then we would sleep through until late afternoon, then quickly eat before being back on stage. At weekends, our working hours were even longer.

There were fights at the club every night. Usually they were between sailors and locals over women. Quite often, we would hear guns going off while we played. It was a very heavy scene. Gary gave us advice about how to handle the audience and what type of music they liked to hear. We were a rowdy raucous band and the Germans loved that. Unfortunately, the club owner didn't. He just wanted us to play pop hits. We soon found out why. He had just bought these amazing new Fender amplifiers. He used to call them his 'boxes' and they were his pride and joy. 'Look after my boxes, boys,' he used to say every night before we went on stage. To be fair, his amps were superb. It was the first time we had used really good equipment. They didn't stop us playing loud though. As soon as we started our set, we would turn them all up to ten because that was what we always did. We were twice as loud as the other act, who played all the straight hits. The boss knew the second we came on. He would charge down to the front of the hall and start screaming that we were ruining his boxes. He'd make us play at a paltry volume. It wasn't our scene, but Gary persuaded us to put up with it if we wanted to get paid.

As it turned out, we didn't get paid, not properly anyway. The owner was trying to keep us happy with dribs and drabs of cash, but after a fortnight, we had hardly made anything. When we complained, he said we didn't deserve any money. 'You're too loud and you don't play enough hits,' he said. It didn't matter that the audience loved our show, he was the boss and he wanted everyone to do what he told them. After three weeks, we knew he wasn't going to pay us properly, so we decided to do a runner back to England. We were skint and, besides, it was a waste of time if we couldn't play what we wanted. We were performing a watered-down version of our set.

By then, we had just enough money to get us back to the ferry. One night, we loaded all our gear into the van, ready to leave, so that the owner wouldn't know we had gone until the next evening. The rest of the band were happy to simply get out of there, but I was determined to get my own back first. I wasn't going to let him get away with not paying us. I tried to think of the worst thing I could do to him. It was obvious. I decided to destroy his beloved amplifiers. That would show him.

My plan was brilliant, even if I say so myself. During the day, the club owner's kids used to play with toy bow and arrows, which they always left lying around. At 4am, having pretended to go to sleep on the stairs, I got up and went to find an arrow. I took a razor blade and put a tiny slit in the cloth on the front of the amps, slipped the arrow though and punctured the speakers. It was a genius idea, because you couldn't tell that they had been tampered with. Then I messed with the fuses. That would make the amps blow up when they were switched on. Only after the fuses had been fixed would anyone realise that the speakers were fucked. We would be long gone by then.

I had thought everything out very carefully, so that we couldn't get caught. At 6am, we got into the van and drove to Holland to catch the ferry. Just as we got to the dock, we saw the ferry pulling out. There was only one boat a day. We were panicking. By then, the club owner would have found out that the amps were broken and would have sent some of his heavies after us. We ran out on to the pier and started screaming and waving our arms at the ferry. As luck would have it, the captain saw us and came back to shore to let us on. He probably saved our lives.

By sheer coincidence, about a month later, Don and I were in London, walking down Oxford Street, when we saw the club owner's right-hand man walking towards us. He was an enormous black guy, a real scary character. Don spotted him first. 'Don't look now, Nod,' he said. 'I think we're going to die.' The pair of us made a dash into Selfridges and managed to avoid him. We found out later from the band that went out to Kiel to replace us that after the amps had blown, the whole show had had to be cancelled and the owner was furious. He was screaming blue murder, saying he wanted us punished. I was delighted. In those days, bands didn't have a legal leg to stand on. If you got ripped off – which happened all the time – you had to use your brain to get your own back. I had done exactly that.

*

In Britain, we were playing four or five gigs a week. Although our biggest fan base was still in the Midlands, there were other places, such as Scotland and Wales, where we had also built up a substantial following. Most of our shows were one-offs – only the big-name bands could afford to tour. Unless we were in Scotland, Wales or the south-west, we drove home every night. The travelling was the toughest part, particularly for me, because if Swin wasn't with us, I had to drive. There weren't many motorways, so we would end up going down little roads or over mountains at 4am in our old J2 van. In the winter, I sometimes couldn't see more than a few yards ahead because of freezing fog or ice on the windows. When it was really cold, the others used to fight over who got to sit in the front. Our van, which we called Betsy, had its engine between the two front seats, so it was always warm there.

Betsy was falling apart. She was held together with rust and string. The floor at the back was caving in with the weight of our equipment and the wheels were knackered from all the long trips on terrible roads. The best thing about that van was the seats. We had ripped out the old ones and replaced them with really comfortable aircraft seats, which we had found in a scrapyard. Dave's dad, Jack Hill, was the only reason Betsy lasted as long as she did. He did all the repairs on her himself. He was great at keeping her on the road and he saved us a fortune in garage bills.

For the first few years of the band, our gigs were booked by an agent called Maurice Jones, who had been looking after the 'N Betweens before I joined. Maurice was also our first manager. He is now a rock promoter. He has his own company, MCP, which he started in the early '70s. When we were with him, he worked for the Astra Agency in Wolverhampton, which handled a lot of Midlands acts. We took him on as our manager because he was a nice guy, although to be honest he didn't know much about managing in those days. In many ways, Maurice was as green as we were, but he liked our band and he put a lot of effort into getting us gigs. We weren't an easy group to represent. We were brash and outrageous on stage, so he had to be careful what venues he booked us into. We were also very loud. We were always getting complaints about the noise, but we refused to turn it down. The other bands at the Astra Agency did traditional pop covers and a bit of comedy. Maurice was the only person there prepared to stick his neck out for us. No one else ever understood what we were about. All they wanted was to get in as much work as possible, so they kept trying to push us in a poppier direction. What we did like about the Astra Agency was that they could get us on bills with some great bands. We were the only group they had who could support the likes of Cream. There was no way they could have put their pop acts on with them.

If we were the black sheep of the agency in England, in Scotland it was a different story. Audiences up there loved rowdy bands. We spent at least one weekend a month in Scotland, either sleeping in the van or basing ourselves at a B&B in Glasgow. A lot of our fans actually thought we were Scottish, because we played there so much. We loved it because the scene seemed a lot trendier than it was in England. Venues liked to take risks with bands who were doing something a bit different. We played with some great groups such as The Dream Police, who later became The Average White Band, and an early incarnation of what went on to become The Sensational Alex Harvey Band. Our Scottish gigs also kept the band afloat, because the promoters paid us in cash. In England, we usually got cheques and we could sometimes wait forever for those to come through with all the con-merchants who were in the business back then.

Some our wildest shows were in Scotland. It was the same in our Slade days. One particular 'N Betweens gig which sticks in my mind was in Cumnock, which is just south of Glasgow. It was a Saturday night and we were playing the town hall, which we later found out was a venue very few bands ever went back to. From the start of our set, the whole crowd was split down the middle, with one half standing on one side of the hall and the other half on the opposite side. There was a big space between them. We couldn't understand it. Just before we were due to finish, the two groups charged at each other. There were dozens of those fold-up chairs stacked at the back of the hall and they were flinging them at each other. It was a real bloodbath. We scarpered off stage and hid in the dressing room. Then the promoter appeared. 'What a brilliant gig,' he said. 'The crowd loved it.' 'So why were they fighting and throwing things?' we asked. 'Oh, don't worry about that. They always throw things when they're having a good time. If they didn't like you, they would have come on stage and trashed your equipment.' The bloke wanted to book us again straight away, but I don't think we ever took him up on his offer.

Our Saturday nights in Scotland usually saw us play two gigs, one in a university, a ballroom or a town hall, then another later in a club. The clubs were almost always in Glasgow and didn't finished until at least 4am. We had a regular B&B there that we stayed in. It was just off Sauchiehall Street. Right across the road was a ballroom called The Electric Garden, which was one of our regular gigs. The resident DJ was Richard Park, who now runs Capital Radio. Unfortunately, the bloke who ran the B&B was ex-army and a real stickler for good behaviour. He wasn't happy that we would roll in at four or five in the morning, so he always got us up for breakfast at 7am. There were usually six of us sleeping in the same room – the band and either two roadies or a couple of mates. The owner would kick us out of bed, march us downstairs and force-feed us porridge. 'Eat it up, boys, it's good for you,' he'd say. 'You've paid for breakfast and you wouldn't want to miss the most important meal of the day.' We'd eat his porridge, then all crawl back to our room for some more kip. They were fantastic days. We had so much fun in Scotland. We made loads of mates there that we kept in touch with for years.

*

I was at home in the Midlands one afternoon when I got a call from Maurice, our agent. He had an offer of work for us, a two-month residency abroad. When he told me where it was, I thought he was joking. I had to get him to repeat it several times before I was sure I had heard him right. Someone wanted us to go to the Bahamas. 'The Bahamas? In the Caribbean? Are you taking the piss?' It turned out he wasn't. A week later, we were on our way there. If it sounds strange now, it seemed unbelievable then. As luck would have it, some bloke from Wolverhampton, who was a big 'N Betweens fan, had gone out to the Bahamas and ended up promoting a club there. He wanted us to fly over and be the resident band for two months. Right up until we had our plane tickets in our hands, we didn't dare believe it. For us, it was a heaven-sent gig. For a start, none of us had ever been anywhere exotic or hot before. It was also a great opportunity for us to get away from the local venues we had been playing non-stop. It would give our audience a bit of a break and mean we would make more impact when we came back. We packed up all our equipment and went out there.

We couldn't believe our eyes when we arrived in the Bahamas. We had never seen anything like it. There were huge reptiles crawling up walls and palm trees every-where. It was paradise, pure paradise. Better still, we were thrown into the lap of luxury. We were staying on Grand Bahama Island and we had been booked into a huge fantastic hotel. We had two bedrooms between the four of us, which we considered high living back then. Both rooms overlooked a marina. There were loads of amazing yachts moored there, including one which belonged to Frank Sinatra. We had to pinch ourselves to make sure we weren't dreaming. Here we were, four scraggy-arsed kids from Wolverhampton, watching from our window to see if Frank and his cronies would turn up. We really thought we had landed on our feet. We were told to order whatever we wanted from room service and the club would pick up the tab. Naturally, we went berserk.

On the first night, the promoter took us to a club which was part of the hotel complex. It was really posh, full of tourists and fabulous suntanned women. Dave, of course, was in his element. On stage was a band from Manchester. The singer was a guy called Red Hoffman, who I last saw as an extra in Coronation Street. The crowd was predominately white. There were a few locals, but mainly it was English and American holidaymakers. 'Is this the sort of place we'll be playing?' we asked the promoter. He nodded. Fantastic – we thought we had died and gone to heaven. The next day, we came back down to earth with a bump. The bloke took us to the real venue we had been booked to play. It was right on the other side of the island, in the black area. It couldn't have been more different from the club we had visited the previous evening. It was out on its own in the middle of a field. From the outside, it looked like a big shack. 'This can't be it,' I said. The promoter nodded, again.

That night, we played our first gig at the venue. We had absolutely no idea what to expect. Our set started at 9pm. For the first three hours, we had been told, the audience would be made up mainly of white tourists. We decided that was when we should play our poppiest songs. We were pretty sure that only chart hits would go down well. 'There's a curfew at midnight,' the promoter told us. 'That's when all the tourists have to return to their hotels. After that, the locals come in.' We were terrified when we heard that. We were sure the locals would hate us. Apparently, they were used to Bahamian bands, who played calypso and ska music. We had visions of being thrown off the island and having to flee back to Wolverhampton.

Our first show started off pretty well. We were right about the tourists wanting to hear hits. Our second set, after the curfew, was to be the real challenge. When we walked back on stage that first night, we could see the shocked look in the eyes of the locals. Not only were we four white kids, but we were wearing our outrageous gear. They didn't know what to make of us. For a second, I thought there was going to be a riot. I looked at Dave and he stared back at me. There was nothing we could do but get on and play.

Before we had even begun, there were shouts of dissent from the crowd. Some of the locals made it clear that they didn't want to watch us. We decided to ignore them and opened the set with a James Brown track. Straight away, the atmosphere changed. Unbeknown to us, James Brown was a god on this island. We later found out that all the jukeboxes in the pubs and clubs were full of soul and Tamla Motown. That was perfect for us. It was what we were playing anyway. The locals couldn't believe their ears. After a couple of songs, people in the front row were literally kissing our feet. Bahamians had never seen anyone actually perform James Brown's music before. Watching a bunch of white guys doing it was astonishing to them. To say we were relieved at their reaction is a gross understatement. We were more shocked than anyone. From that night on, we packed the place out.

If we had some weird experiences later in our career with Slade, our stint in the Bahamas prepared us for them. We ended up with the most bizarre show you can imagine. The idea was that we would not only play our own music, but also back a lot of local acts, which included limbo dancers, a couple of fire-eaters and a transvestite go-go dancer in a cage. It was like an Acid-inspired cabaret show. The compere was a gay guy called Eric. He was a local, well-known and well-loved, but totally nuts. We had never met a really outrageous gay bloke before. We had seen quite a few gay acts when we played in Germany, but they were positively tame compared to Eric. He was like a black Larry Grayson, but much more over the top. He had a huge Afro and he was always stoned out of his tree. Besides being the compere, he played the bongos. Everyone in that club claimed to have a special musical talent and, at some point in the evening, most of them would want to get on stage with us. Eric always said that he was the second-best bongo player in the Bahamas, so we had to put up with him playing a twenty-minute bongo set every night. Once he came on, we couldn't get him off. God knows who was the best bongo player in the Bahamas. We never found that out. We just presumed that once Eric had seen someone who he thought was better than him.

It was Eric who got me stoned for the first time. He used to have a bottle of rum in his flat that he had spiked with marijuana. He'd soak the weed in it, like you put herbs in vinegar to give it flavour. Then he'd bring the rum to the club and offer me a drink of it. I'd be out of my tree on one rum and coke. For ages, I didn't know why.

I couldn't make up most of the madness that went on in the Bahamas. Not a single night passed without us ending up in at least one ludicrous situation. Eric was often so off his head that I had to take over as compere. I was also the scenery shifter and I brought on the go-go dancer's cage. I did everything. I was either throwing ego-freaks off stage when they wouldn't leave – a bloke called Prince Badu was the worst for that – or I was dragging stoned musicians out of the bar when it was supposed to be their slot. I remember the time we let the bloke who did the door of the club get up and sing with us. He was a huge man mountain, unbelievably big. For weeks, he had hassled us to bring him on stage. When we finally let him sing, his voice was like that of a little squeaky mouse. The four of us literally fell over laughing. He was built like a brick shithouse, but he sang like a four-year-old on helium.

Another great moment involved the Silver Man. He was one of the local cabaret acts who came on during the first part of our show. He was called the Silver Man because he covered himself from head to toe in silver paint. He walked on and did a sort of voodoo dance. That was his act. He had to time his performance very carefully so he could finish in time to wash the paint off. If he kept it on too long, his skin couldn't breathe and he would pass out. One night, Eric was playing his bongo set, boring everyone to tears, as usual. He was so stoned that he wouldn't stop. I could see the Silver Man standing behind a curtain at the side of the stage. He was waving at me to get Eric off before his paint dried. Suddenly, I looked round and he had fainted. There was a trail of silver paint all down the curtain and he was crumpled in a heap on the floor. For one awful moment, I thought he was dead. I rushed over, washed his paint off and he woke up, thank God. That's what it was like every night. We were working with loonies.

Once every couple of weeks, the club flew in soul artists from the States as special guests. One night, we turned up to find William Bell in our dressing room. He had just had a huge hit with Judy Clay called 'Private Number'. He was great. He sang with us as his backing band. He also brought his own guitarist, who was amazing. He was only young, but I swear he could play just like Jimi Hendrix. Another night, we had to support a girl group called The Twans. They were three gorgeous black girls, basically a cheap-skate Supremes. In the afternoon, we sat in the dressing room and rehearsed their whole set with them. It was only four or five numbers. That evening, they started the show with a cover of Aretha Franklin's 'Respect'. They came on stage wearing matching white Supremes-style gowns and big Afro wigs and launched into their choreographed dance routine. What no one knew was that the lead singer had lost her voice between the rehearsal in the afternoon and the show. She had been too scared to tell anyone. The backing girls went 'Woo' , after which she was supposed to sing 'What you want'. Instead, there was silence. The others went 'Woo' again. Still nothing. The lead singer was opening her mouth, but no sound was coming out. Suddenly, this bloke in the front row of the audience shouted, 'Sing it like it is, sister.' We just collapsed. The girls were still doing their dance, but the four of us were on the floor, laughing. Every gig was like that, total chaos. It was frightening really, but also great fun.

Probably my fondest memory of the Bahamas involved Dave in a dress. All the way through the band's career, Dave liked to hang out with groups of girls. He was well in touch with his feminine side even then. He would go shopping with them and sit and chitter-chatter to them for hours about hair, clothes and make-up. They loved him for it. After a couple of weeks in the Bahamas, Dave had made friends with a load of American and English girls. One afternoon, they took him to a fashion show which was happening at one of the other hotels on the island. How it came about I have no idea, because he never told us, but Dave ended up as one of the catwalk models. He wasn't modelling men's clothes, though. He was wearing a dress. He came back to the club that night in it. It was a full-length floral thing, all pink and white. He just wandered in with all his girl cronies, boasting that his picture was going to be in the Bahamian newspaper the next day. We were flabbergasted. It got worse. 'I'm keeping the dress on for the show,' announced Dave. Jim hit the roof. For once though, Dave did have an excuse. You couldn't wear much clobber on stage because it was so hot and he insisted that a dress was a cool alternative to trousers. I'll give it to him, he got a great reaction. We hadn't been on stage two minutes when a girl in the audience stormed up to Dave. She was pointing at him, shouting, 'My dress. My dress.' She was furious because Dave was wearing exactly the same outfit as her.

Just as we were settling into our luxurious new lifestyle, disaster struck. Once again, we discovered that we weren't going to be paid. The promoter had given us only dribs and drabs of our money, but we hadn't worried. At the time, we didn't need it. We were living in a fabulous hotel, ordering all our food on room service and getting our drinks for free, courtesy of the club – or so we thought. Little did we know that the club was in big financial trouble. Halfway through our two-month residency, the owner did a runner. He left our hotel and bar bill unpaid. It was thousands of pounds. We had probably £100 between us, but the hotel insisted that we pay the full amount. Our only hope was that a new owner would reopen the club. Fortunately, that was what happened. The hotel moved us into one of their staff apartments and took half of our wages each week until we had paid off the bill. We were there for the next three months. That's how long it took to pay it off. The hotel was good about it, because they could see we were at least making an effort, but it was a big comedown for us. The four of us were sharing one tiny room and we had next to no money for food. We used to go to the lunchtime buffets at the hotels in town where you could eat as much as you liked for a couple of dollars, then not eat for the next twenty-four hours.

On our occasional nights off, we had parties in our little room. We had made friends with a lot of local kids, most of whom were from wealthy British and American families. They would come round with booze and food they had smuggled out of their parents' houses. They also brought lots of records with them. Most were hits in America, but had yet to be released in Britain. Suddenly, we had access to a huge source of new material, months before any of our contemporaries back home. The kids were delighted to lend us their records. We would learn songs like 'Born To Be Wild' by Steppenwolf, then play them as requests on stage.

We came back from the Bahamas a different band. For a start, the four of us were much closer. It was a very telling period. It was the first time we had spent so much time together. We lived, ate and slept in one room. The set-up was a nightmare and we had blazing rows. I'm a Gemini, so I have two totally different sides. I can fly off the handle, but only if there's a reason for it. I prefer to talk people round rather than shout at them, so it takes a lot for me to lose my rag. However, if I do snap, I have a horrendous temper. The others all learnt quickly that it was a waste of time to row with me. None of them could ever get the better of me in an argument.

During those last weeks in the Bahamas, we got what we didn't like about each other out of our systems, which helped us a lot later down the line. We discovered that we were four very different characters. Jim was probably the most argumentative. He could also be really insulting, although half the time, he didn't even realise it. His mouth worked faster than his brain. I remember him meeting a girl once and telling her her hair looked like straw. Naturally, she was furious. We never knew if he was trying to insult people or if he just didn't think, but after spending so much time together, we got used to it. When he made insulting remarks to the rest of us, we just ignored him. We learnt that, in a band, you couldn't take each other too seriously or you'd just split up.

Musically, there was a dramatic improvement in us, too. Four months of non-stop shows had made us incredibly tight. It was particularly fantastic for Don. Dave, Jim and I always took a few breaks during the evening when the local acts came on. Unfortunately, very few of them had their own drummer, so Don would end up playing straight through from 9pm to 4am every night. The biggest difference in the band, however, was our set. Previously, we had been playing mainly Motown, R'n'B and a bit of pop. We hadn't ventured much into other styles of music. After the Bahamas, our repertoire totally changed. We had hours-worth of new material that no one at home had heard, because it hadn't been released there yet. When those songs were released in Britain, our fans went crazy. They loved the fact that they already knew all the words. 'Born To Be Wild' was the song that we were particularly associated with, because we always closed our show with a really raucous version of it.

Shortly after our Bahamas trip, the band got a new agent. We were tempted away from the Astra Agency by a bloke called Roger Allen. He and his business partner, Nita Anderson, had just formed a new agency in the Midlands. Roger was in some ways, like a '60s version of Del Boy. He was a real wheeler-dealer. Everyone in Wolverhampton knew him. He had promoted venues and ballroom gigs for years, but mainly he managed bands like The Montanas and The Californians. He always got his groups great deals, because he was such a blagger. He's still the same today. The last I heard, he was living in Tenerife selling time-shares. He was a fabulous fun bloke, but a terror. He always seemed to be owing everyone money. We loved him to bits and he loved our band. He knew we were good and that we had potential, although he was never quite sure what to do with us. Unlike the Astra Agency, however, he wanted us to stay as we were. He looked on us as a challenge, rather than a liability.

For all Roger's faults, he turned out to be a great agent. Not long after he took us on, he managed to blag us an audition in London with Fontana Records. He knew the MD, Jack Baverstock, because he had just done a deal with the label for one of his other acts. Roger set up a meeting at Fontana's head office in Marble Arch. 'Jack's a massive 'N Betweens fan,' he told us. 'He's wanted to meet you for ages.' We later found out that was total nonsense. It was a typical Roger scam, but as usual, it worked. He got us in to see the MD, not some A&R guy, and it turned out to be our big break.

I'll never forget the first time we walked into Jack Baverstock's office. I'm sure none of the others will either. It was enormous, full of plush furniture and paintings. We had never seen anything like it. Jack was there with an Australian actor, who at the time was the face of the Barratt Homes TV adverts. The pair of them were playing golf on the carpet. They had one of those stick-up golf holes and they were practising their putting. 'Come in and sit down,' said Jack, without even looking up at us. Then he started talking business while still hitting his shots. He said straight away that he was going to give us some studio time. 'I want you guys to record for a week with an engineer,' he said. 'Just get down some of the songs you play on stage. After that, I'll decide what to do with you.' We couldn't believe our ears. We had only ever spent a few half days in studios. How Roger had blagged all this, I never found out, not even after Jack later admitted that he had never heard of the 'N Betweens before.

The following week, we began recording in a studio in the basement of the Fontana building. It was the studio that Paul Weller took over many years later and called Solid Bond. We went in there every day from 9am to 6pm. We wrote two or three songs of our own, all basic bluesy jams, but mostly we played our favourite songs from our set. We knew nothing about the technical side of a studio, we left that to the engineer. Jack would come down once a day for five or ten minutes to check up on us. At the end of the week, he announced that he was going to release our songs as an album. We were knocked out. We thought we had just been doing demos. Moreover, we had recorded a real mish-mash of material. There were tracks by Frank Zappa, The Moody Blues, Jeff Lynne and a couple of Tamla Motown classics. Some were heavy rock, others ballads. There was no consistent style , but that was what Jack loved. 'Never in my life have I heard such a schizophrenic set,' he told us.

Before we could release our album, we had to change our name. Jack insisted on it. He said he didn't like the 'N Betweens. 'It's makes you sound like you're bisexual,' he said. We freaked out. That had never even crossed our minds. In the '60s, if you were gay, it was a real scandal. No one came out of the closet, not in pop music anyway. It just wasn't acceptable. We suggested a few names of our own, including Knicky Knacky Noo, but Jack hated all of them. His idea was Ambrose Slade. 'What the hell does that mean?' we asked him. He told us it had come from his secretary. Apparently, she gave everything she owned a name. For example, her handbag was Arnold and her watch was John, or whatever. Don't ask me why, please, because I never got to the bottom of it. She also named everything on her desk, like her notepad, her pens, even the office stapler. I never found out exactly what each of those objects was called, but one of them was called Ambrose and another one Slade. Jack had seen them lying side by side on her desk and come up with our new name. You can imagine the arguments the four of us had about this. We thought Ambrose Slade sounded ridiculous, but we were desperate for a proper record deal. We had yet to have our first hit single and we knew that releasing an album would blow everyone away in the Midlands. We would have done anything to keep Jack happy. There was no way we were going to risk missing out on our big chance. After drowning our reservations in a dozen beers, we became Ambrose Slade.

The second thing Jack insisted we do was get a London agent. In those days, all bands broke out of London, because that was where the entire record industry was based. Even though The Beatles were from Liverpool and The Hollies from Manchester, they had only cracked it after going to London. Midlands agents could get groups a few gigs in the capital, but not in the important venues. To play places where members of the music press might see you and to get support slots with big-name bands, you had to have a London agent. For us, that was a problem. Roger was our agent and he was the one who had taken us to Fontana in the first place. We told Jack that we weren't willing to just drop Roger, but he told us not to worry. We later found out that Roger and Nita had been given a £300 pay-off! The next thing we knew, we not only had a new agent, but a new very famous manager.

The agent was a guy called John Gunnell. He and his brother, Rick, were part of a big London agency who handled dozens of R'n'B and soul acts like Georgie Fame, Alan Price and Geno Washington and The Ram Jam Band. They also owned a number of very hip London clubs, where all their artists played. The pair of them were well-known tough guys in the business, but they were perfect for us and so were their venues. Jack had sent John Gunnell a tape of some of our songs and he wanted to meet us. We knew how important he was and what a big deal it would be if he took us on. When he arrived at Fontana, he looked like a typical London agent, very dapper and smartly dressed. He had brought Chas Chandler with him. Chas was six foot six and well-built. We recognised him the moment he walked through the door. He had been the bassist in The Animals and he had discovered and produced Jimi Hendrix. We were in awe.

Chas and John came to the studio to listen to our album, which by then had been given the title *Beginnings*. We could tell they were impressed. Like Jack, they loved the fact that all of the tracks were so different. Straight away, John said, 'I want to take you on. From now on, I'm your agent. I'll fix you up with some London dates.' Chas said that he wanted to see us play live. We had no idea why he was so interested. No one had even told us why he was there. We later found out that Hendrix had gone back to the States and that Chas was looking for a new act to manage. He and John had just set up a management company as part of the Robert Stigwood Organisation. Robert Stigwood was one of the biggest names in the business. He looked after the likes of The Bee Gees and Eric Clapton. The only act Chas and John had so far was Noel Redding's new band and they were looking to sign someone else. After hearing our album, they decided that it was a toss-up between us and another band called Trapeze. By sheer coincidence, Trapeze were also from Wolverhampton. All of the members had previously been in different Roger Allen-managed bands which had split up. They had got together in a sort of Wolverhampton supergroup. We had seen Trapeze play and we knew they were good. They were a lot like the Moody Blues – nothing like us.

The first gig that John got us was at a basement club called Rasputins in New Bond Street. It was a strange place for us to play. It was more of a disco than a rock venue and it was very trendy. We were almost at the end of our first set when Chas turned up. The place wasn't packed by any means, but it was obvious that the people who were there loved us. Disco crowds were notoriously hard to impress. They tended to ignore the band and just dance to the music. They thought that showing any outward signs of appreciation made them look uncool.

By the time Chas arrived, everyone was watching. I was giving it my all. I had pulled out every trick I knew to get the audience involved. I had people on stage singing with us and I was picking out the best-looking girls to wind up between songs. The reaction was brilliant. The club was going berserk. Nearly everyone was jumping around and shouting. We had saved our best numbers for the final half-hour, because we had guessed that Chas wouldn't turn up until late. As soon as we saw him, we knew we had cracked it. He was standing at the back with a huge grin on his face.

After the show, Chas came into the dressing room and announced that that he wanted to sign us. 'You're a breath of fresh air,' he said. 'I've never seen a disco crowd so excited.' He claimed then that he had made his decision the moment he walked through the door, before he had even seen us on stage. 'I could feel the atmosphere from the top of the stairs.' Years later, he told me a different story. He said that my voice and the way I handled the audience were the main reasons he chose us over Trapeze.

HAIR 'EM
SCARE 'EM

5

Beginnings was in the can and ready for release. All that was needed was a cover shot for the sleeve. Fontana decided it should feature the four of us and sent a photographer up to the Midlands to take our picture. The bloke had obviously been scouting the area for locations and immediately whisked us off to a place called Pouk Hill, which was just round the corner from my house. Pouk Hill was a big old disused quarry and it did look dramatic. It was the middle of winter and the ground was covered in snow.

I was imagining a moody scenic shot with us in the foreground, but as soon as we got there, the photographer said, 'Take off your shirts, lads.' 'But it's bloody freezing,' we moaned. We weren't about to argue with him though. He was the professional and we were a little local band, who he had probably never heard of. We stripped off to the waist. 'Lie down in the snow,' he said next. So we lay down. Our heads were right on the edge of the quarry, which could have made for a great photo. We couldn't believe it when we saw the end-product. The sleeve was just a head shot. You couldn't see the quarry or any snow. It had been a complete waste of time. We wrote a song about that photo session on the next album. By then we were a lot wiser. At the start, we didn't question anything. We did as we were told, because we naively thought the record company knew best.

Beginnings didn't sell very well, but it was a good album considering it was our first effort and it had only taken a week to record. Having it out helped us get better gigs for more money, so we were happy, but the suits at Fontana were a bit disappointed. They hadn't expected it to be a monster hit, but they had hoped it would chart. Fortunately, the album market then wasn't the be-all and end-all it is today. You could be a popular act and make money just from hit singles.

Chas wasn't phased at all by the album's lack of commercial success. Like us, he was a singles fanatic and he knew from the start that was where our strength lay. 'You could be the kings of the short pop song', he would tell us. We agreed. We knew we had something different to offer in that area. In the late '60s, most guitar bands were hippies who played half-hour solos. We preferred three- or four-minute-long party tracks.

After the album came out, we concentrated on playing live as much as possible, particularly in London. Getting a new agent had been a good move. Suddenly, we were being booked to play places like The Red Car Jazz Club, which was a well-known rock venue. We even made our debut at The Marquee club, a very prestigious gig. Yes were doing a residency there and we were to support them. They were fantastic. In those days, they did rock versions of songs from *West Side Story* and Beatles covers. I remember standing at the side of the stage, watching them and thinking, 'I've just played to that crowd.' I couldn't believe that we were on at The Marquee. For years, we had been coming down to London to see groups like Jethro Tull, Free and The Who play there.

The trendiest venues we played were The Bag O' Nails and The Speakeasy. John, our agent, owned The Bag O' Nails, so we had a foot in the door there. Everyone who was anyone went to these clubs to drink after hours. You'd meet other bands, journalists, industry people and loads of famous faces. They were tiny, but they were the places to be seen in. The first time we played The Speakeasy, the manager came over and said, 'Frank Zappa has asked if you would join him at his table.' We were gobsmacked. We had been covering his songs for years. We sat down with him and he told us he loved our set.

Another of our regular London gigs was an all-night R'n'B club called The Temple in Wardour Street. Geno Washington and Georgie Fame had played there in the early days, when it was called The Flamingo. We often did a set at The Marquee, then went on stage at The Temple at around three in the morning. To make it financially viable for us to come down from the Midlands, we had to play a few places in one night. Bands didn't earn much from The Marquee. You played it for the prestige.

Some of my favourite gigs were private parties. Because we had joined this big agency, we were often asked to play at posh events. One time, we were booked to play at a film-wrap party at a castle in Herefordshire. It was a real Hollywood affair. The film had been directed by Jerry Lewis and it starred Sammy Davis Jnr and Peter Lawford from the Sinatra Rat Pack. We had never done anything like it before. After our first set, Sammy Davis came over to meet us. 'I really enjoyed the show,' he said. 'Can I get up and sing with you later.' We were like bumbling idiots. 'Er, yeah,' we muttered. Sammy came on stage for a couple of numbers. I was amazed. I stood there, playing the guitar, trying to act cool, thinking, 'Oh my God, I'm on stage with Sammy Davis.' Afterwards, he was asking us all about music. He was just a normal bloke, really friendly, which surprised me. He was the first world-famous film star I had ever met. We sat and got pissed with him. I was in awe, but I wasn't star-stuck. I never have been. I do remember thinking, 'Thank God it's not Frank Sinatra.' I don't think I could have coped had it been Frank.

One of the first things Chas did after taking us on was hire us a press agent. He got a bloke called Keith Altham, who was an ex-writer on the *NME*. Keith was a big name in PR – he did The Rolling Stones, The Who and The Moody Blues. He had been friends with Chas in his Animals days and we knew from reading his *NME* features that he had hung out a lot with The Beatles.

One day, Chas and Keith were discussing our image and how to market the band. None of us was there. The problem was that although our hippyish style had been unusual in the Midlands, in London, lots of bands wore similar clothes and had the same long hair. 'The best way to make them stand out from other bands is to shave all their hair off and make them look like skinheads,' said Keith. He was joking, of course. But it was like a red rag to a bull to Chas. As soon as the words came out of Keith's mouth, a light went on in Chas' head. 'Keith, you've cracked it.' Keith couldn't believe Chas had taken him seriously. Chas meant it alright. The only catch now was to try and sell the idea to us. 'No way!' That was our unanimous reaction to Chas' suggestion. Dave in particular was horrified. He loved his long hair and no one was going to cut it off, not even Chas. Besides, we had been slowly building up our following and we weren't going to change overnight for anyone. We had other worries too. The skinhead look may have been more of a fashion statement than linked to a political movement in those days, but it was very much associated with violence. That wasn't our thing. We did sometimes play to skinheads, but we weren't part of that scene.

Chas called us into his office to try and talk us round. He was one persuasive guy, I'll give him that. 'It's a great idea,' he kept saying. 'I know it'll work. No other bands are doing it. You guys will stick out like a sore thumb. It's exactly what you need.' He gave us every argument under the sun. We went in there adamant that he wouldn't change our minds, but we went away thinking that it might, in fact, be a good idea. We could always be swayed by Chas. He had been through the mill with Hendrix and so we trusted his judgement. Eventually, we agreed to go for the chop. Dave was the hardest to convince. Ultimately though, if he thought there was money in it at the end of the day, Dave could be pressured into anything.

Chas arranged for us to get our hair cut by a bloke in Soho called Harry. He had done Hendrix's hair. In fact, he had invented Hendrix's haircut. That was all Chas' idea, too. Not many people knew it, but Chas had brought Hendrix to London, decided to change his look and taken him to Harry to give him an Afro. It was probably Chas telling us that which had convinced us to become skinheads.

Harry Hair – as we immediately christened him – was delighted at the prospect of shaving our heads. Dave's terror no doubt egged him on. Dave and Jimmy absolutely dreaded the prospect. Dave was unbelievably proud of his hair. I wasn't too bothered, so I went first. Don went next, then Jim, then Dave. It was horrendous watching Dave's face as his long locks fell to the floor. 'I can't look,' he kept saying. 'What are the girls going to think?' He was fighting back the tears. In the end, neither Dave nor Jim got the full crop – they both had an inch or so of hair left.

Afterwards, all four of us looked awful. We were horrors. I quite liked it though, as did Don. The pair of us looked really hard. We felt hard too, which was quite a buzz. We gave ourselves nicknames to suit our new look. I was The Pink Head, because my hair was naturally blonde, so I looked like I was bald. Don was dark and stubbly and looked like he had 7 o' clock shadow all the time, so we called him The Blue Head. Dave wouldn't have stood for a nickname. He hated being a skinhead. He was so uncomfortable without his long hair.

Straight after our trip to Harry's, Chas took us to buy new outfits. Skinheads wore Ben Sherman shirts with braces, turned-up jeans and big bovver boots, so that's what we got. At the time, it was just a fashion for young kids. No groups actually dressed like that. As soon as we changed into the gear, we were transformed. Chas was delighted. 'Didn't I tell you it would work?' he said. He was right.

A few days later, I went back to the Midlands. I was still living with my parents, although I was rarely home. I didn't get to our house until 3am, so I went straight to bed. My mum and dad knew nothing about my new look. The next morning, my mum came in to wake me up. The first thing she saw was a pair of huge Doc Marten boots at the end of the bed. Then she noticed my bald head on the pillow. She freaked. She didn't realise it was me. She was screaming, 'Get up! Who are you?' When I woke up and turned round, she was gobsmacked. 'What have you done to your lovely long curly hair?' She hated my skinhead.

Our first new publicity pictures came out in the *NME*. They were full-length shots of the four of us, standing separately in different poses. For the first time, we were billed as Slade, not Ambrose Slade. Chas had never liked the name Ambrose Slade. 'It's not catchy enough. You need something snappier.' He had said that since day one. Whenever we played, promoters always got our name wrong. We'd been billed as Arnold Shake, Amgo Slake, every misspelling imaginable. Sometimes they got the Slade part right, but never Ambrose. 'From now on, you're simply Slade,' said Chas, which suited us fine. We had never liked Ambrose Slade ourselves. I have to hand it to Chas, the change of name and the new look could not have been more effective. The *NME* shots were striking. Suddenly, we were getting loads of attention, just for being these supposed hard guys. It was very controversial. Writers were saying that we would encourage violence at gigs. It's hard to imagine now, but the idea of a skinhead group shocked people.

Over the next few weeks, everyone we met was stunned by our appearance. All our pals thought we were mad. Our fans in the Midlands agreed. 'You looked so much better before. Grow your hair back.' When we walked on stage at shows, the audiences couldn't believe their eyes. The first few rows would be standing there with their mouths wide open. Even people who had seen the publicity shots were speechless. I don't think they believed we really looked like that. In the end, the fans got used to it, but very few of them ever liked it.

One night, we played a university gig in Manchester. In those days, unis and colleges regularly put on all-nighter events. There would be maybe a dozen bands playing in three or four different halls. One hall would host the folky acts, another the progressive rock bands, another the pop groups. That night, we were playing with bands like Atomic Rooster and Stone The Crows, most of whom we had played with many times before. Everyone was sharing the same big dressing room. When we walked in, the room went silent. It was like one of those old Westerns, when the stranger walks into the bar and eveyone immediately stops talking and stares. Most of the other groups knew us and knew what we were like, but suddenly they were scared shitless of us. It was like that wherever we went. People always knew Slade had arrived. It was exactly what Chas had wanted. We were still playing the same songs at the same venues, but now everyone knew who we were.

We had imagined that press interest in us would die down after people got used to our look. We were wrong. It went mad. Writers didn't know what to make of us. They liked our music – the reviews were almost always good – but they hated our image. At least, they hated what they thought our image stood for. They didn't realise it was only a fashion thing. Most music journalists were based in London and they hadn't seen us in the 'N Betweens, so they thought we were real tough nuts. I mean, we were in our own way, particularly me and Don. We were true working-class and we quite liked being thought of as hard guys. It had its advantages, too. We never once had any trouble getting paid at venues. Promoters were always trying to fleece bands in those days. But not us. Not anymore.

Despite our notoriety, we never went looking for trouble. Sometimes, though, trouble found us. The problems started when we began being booked into skinhead venues or when skinheads turned up at our shows. Slowly, they were infiltrating our audience. That was a bit dodgy for the people who had followed us for years. It was also weird for us, because we weren't playing their type of music. Skinheads liked ska, reggae and bluebeat, but only proper black Jamaican acts, like Desmond Deckker and The Aces and Prince Buster, were doing that.

One night at Guildford Civic Hall, the crowd was all

skinheads. There was a really heavy atmosphere all the way through the show. You could feel violence brewing. Afterwards, we were loading our gear into the van, getting ready to set off, when this gang of skinheads came walking towards us. There must have been forty or fifty of them. We had always been wary of a fight breaking out, so we had taken to carrying a rifle in the van as protection. It was just an air rifle and it wasn't loaded. I don't know if the skinheads hadn't enjoyed the show or if they were just out for a fight. We didn't wait around to find out. We threw the rest of the equipment into the back of the van, jumped in and locked the doors. I grabbed the rifle, wound the window down and pretended I was about to shoot at them. You've never seen a gang of skinheads scarper so fast in your life. It was comical. They were running in all directions, screaming. I wished I had had a camera. We were all chanting, 'Fuck off, you arseholes.'

After *Beginnings* came out, Chas moved us from Fontana to Polydor. Both came under the Phillips umbrella. He had worked closely with Polydor in his Hendrix days and he knew all the staff, so he felt more comfortable with them. For our second album, Chas wanted us to start writing our own songs, but before we began work on that, we were to bring out a couple of singles. Chas was keen that we have a hit before releasing another album. The first single was called 'Wild Winds Are Blowing'. Chas met up with us one day and said, 'I've found a song that's perfect for Slade.' He had been sent it by a publishing company. It was a good pop-rock song, not too commercial. It was really our first proper single, although we had released two tracks from *Beginnings*, neither of which was ever going to be a hit.

To promote 'Wild Winds Are Blowing', we made our first TV appearance. It was on *The Alan Price Show*. Alan Price had been the keyboard player in The Animals and he had had a couple of solo hits before being given his own TV series. We got a great reception from the audience. A lot of them had heard about us and were dying to see what we really looked like. We also performed a version of 'Martha My Dear' by The Beatles with Jim playing electric violin. You can imagine the sight of a bunch of skinheads playing this sweet Beatles song. Years later, when I was guest-presenting *Top Of The Pops*, Ric Blaxill, who was then the producer, got me a copy of that show on video. I have to admit, I looked awful. I must have been nervous, but I looked so cocksure. It's the one clip that's always shown when TV programmes do those 'before they were famous' spots.

Our second TV appearance was on *Top Of The Pops*. It was for our next single, 'Shape of Things to Come'. It wasn't a hit, but in those days you could get on the show as a band with a new release. Elton John was on with us. It was his first time on *Top Of The Pops* too. He was performing 'Lady Samantha'. We already knew Elton because we had supported him a couple of times at art colleges in London. Before he got his group together, he had been working for a publisher called Dick James in Denmark Street. He was basically a session musician, who played on those compilation albums they used to sell in Woolworths, with covers of all the pop hits of the day. I remember being quite jealous of Elton that day. He had all his glamourous gear on, while we were looking like thugs. Dave was probably annoyed because he thought Elton would end up pulling all the girls. How wrong can you be?

After 'Shape of Things to Come', we began work on the new album, *Play It Loud*. Chas took us to Olympic Studios in Barnes, a fantastic place, just outside London. He liked to record there because it was where he had done a lot of the Hendrix stuff. The Stones and The Who used it a lot too. We hadn't planned to do the whole album there because of the cost, but the owners had just built a second, much smaller studio next door and offered us a cheap rate to test it out. We more or less lived there for the next two or three weeks.

Chas insisted that the four of us write at least half of the tracks on *Play It Loud*. There was never any question of whether or not we could write a hit. Chas took it for granted that we could. 'You just need practice. Once you've hit on the right formula, it'll be easy.' Dave and I teamed up to write, as did Jim and Don. We hadn't thought much about writing partnerships. Dave and I were the guitarists, so it seemed the most obvious way. It was our first serious attempt at songwriting. To be honest, we were just experimenting. We had no idea where to start. We didn't have a clue what sort of sound we were looking for. We asked Chas for advice. 'Forget complex arrangements. You're a basic gutsy rock'n'roll band, so write basic gutsy rock'n'roll songs.' It was the best thing he could have said. In the past, we had tried to be too smart for our own good. We often chose complicated songs to cover just to prove that we could play them. It was all very clever and arty-farty, but it wasn't us.

Recording the album was a testing time for us, because it had to be finished in three weeks. All bands churned records out in those days. Only The Beatles and The Stones got six months in the studio. Our songs were okay, but it was obvious that they weren't potential commercial hits. There was always something missing. 'Just keep at it,' Chas would say. 'Practice is the key.' He told us that Jimi Hendrix had become the best guitarist in the world by playing twenty-four hours a day. 'I never saw Jimi without a guitar in his hands. When he went for a shit, that guy took his guitar with him. It wasn't just his talent that made him famous. It was hard work.'

As with Hendrix, Chas not only managed us, he pro-duced us too. We had never had a producer other than Kim Fowley and he was just off-the-wall and waved the odd direction at us. Chas was our first proper producer. He sat and listened from the control room, then came into the studio and commented on the arrangements. He made us work on the sound until it was right. He had great ears for spotting a hit. He did it with 'Hey Joe', Hendrix's first hit single.

When Chas discovered Hendrix, he was playing in a

little club in Greenwich Village in New York. Keith Richard had told Chas to go and check him out. Chas brought Hendrix to London and made him over completely, just as he was doing with us. It was he who suggested that Jimi record 'Hey Joe'. We trusted Chas because we knew he had invested everything he had in Hendrix. He reckoned that the Animals had been badly ripped off and he had left the band with very little money. Chas told us that the day before 'Hey Joe' went in the charts, he had sold his last guitar to survive.

Play It Loud came out in 1970. Although it was our second album, it was our first as Slade. By then, we had begun to ease ourselves away from the skinhead scene. On the album cover, we still had our shaved heads, but we made a point of not looking too heavy. I wore a '30s-style flat cap and a checked jacket that was too big for me. The idea was to make ourselves look more acceptable. A lot of venues wouldn't touch us with a barge pole. It was the same with TV shows. If they took the chance with us, it was always fine, but there was still the perception that we were associated with violence.

Play It Loud sold reasonably well and got good reviews, but it didn't chart. We released a single from it called 'Know Who You Are', which was one of our own songs. When it didn't make the charts, frustration started to set in. We couldn't understand why we weren't more popular by then. We had been with Chas for two years, slogging our guts out and still we hadn't had a hit. We had built up a huge live following and we were getting lots of press. It was a puzzle. To his credit, Chas was 100 per cent confident it would happen for us eventually. 'We just need the right record,' he'd say. 'I have every faith in you. Just wait and see.' Other people in the industry didn't agree. We'd hear them say to Chas, 'Slade are never going to break through. Let them go and don't waste your time.' That would infuriate Chas. Whenever anyone made a negative remark, he would go mad. He was a big bloke and he could tear your head off. People rarely said bad things about us more than once to Chas, put it that way.

We took heart from the fact that we were earning good money from gigs. You can't get too despondent when you're packing out venues every night. We were selling out 1,500-capacity shows, which was more than some of the hit bands were doing. People were coming out of curiosity, then coming back because they loved us. It was such a shock for them to see this horrible looking group, then find out that we could play really well. Besides, there were a lot of great live bands, like Stone The Crows, who never had hits. Even the likes of Status Quo, who were a name band, weren't getting into the charts. You didn't have to have hits to get good gigs either. We were playing rock clubs, while the big pop acts were doing ballrooms – it was a totally different circuit with the kind of crowds we wanted. When groups had hits, they got all the screaming girls. That wasn't our bag. We wanted to be popular, but we also wanted fans who were into the music. We wanted to have fun with our audience.

The success of our live show gave Chas the idea for our next single. 'You have to capture what you have on stage in the studio,' he told us. 'If you can do that, you'll have a hit.' As soon as the words came out his mouth, it was obvious what we should do – release our best live track as a single. So that's what we did. For almost two years, we had been ending our set with a Little Richard cover called 'Get Down and Get With It'. It was a very basic twelve-bar blues track, but it had something magical about it. Audiences loved it and it always tore the place apart. It was a storming song to finish with and it somehow summed up what Slade were all about. Little Richard's original was all piano and sax, but our version was much heavier, all powerhouse guitars. Chas loved it. It was the obvious choice for a single.

The skinhead connection was a big part of 'Get Down and Get With It'. Although a lot of skinheads weren't into the type of music we were playing, they all loved our raw rocky sound. They used to stamp their feet in time to our songs. They developed a sort of dance called the moon stomp, which became an integral part of our act. There was a line in the first verse that went 'Everybody raise your hands in the air'. When I sang it, the whole audience would clap their hands above their heads. In the second verse, I'd sing 'Let me hear you stamp your feet' and they'd all do that. It was perfect for skinheads because they wore such big boots. Venues used to shake.

We knew it would be hard to capture the spirit of 'Get Down and Get With It' in the studio. Chas came up with the answer. 'Just play it like you do on stage. Blast it out like it's live and pretend that there's an audience in there with you.' So we went into Olympic and recorded it like that. It was a very simple song, just three chords. We got it right on the first take. It was a one-take wonder. Because of technical constraints, the song was nowhere near as heavy as it was at our gigs. The equipment couldn't cope with it. We played it as loud as we could though and added a great rock'n'roll piano part.

'There's still something missing,' said Chas when we'd finished. 'We need the hand-clapping and the boot-stamping you get at gigs.' That was easily solved. There was a big stairwell outside the studio which was really echoey. We set the mics up out there, then recorded the four of us clapping our hands and stamping our feet. We overdubbed and overdubbed it, so it sounded like it was recorded in a huge hall with a mass of people. It was exactly what Chas had been after.

When 'Get Down and Get With It' was first sent to radio stations, a lot of jocks wouldn't play it because it was so rowdy. A few picked up on it though, including John Peel. It began to get regular plays, then very slowly it started to sell. We were so excited. Until then, we hadn't had much radio play. We had done a few sessions for Radio 1 and played live on several shows. They had a rule then that stations could only play so many records a day, so loads of the music you heard was live. Every lunchtime there was a show called the *Radio 1 Club*, which came live from a venue around the country, and we had done that a lot. Having our single played was a different matter entirely. Every time one of us heard it, we would call the others up. 'Turn on Radio 1! We're on again.' It was our first real taste of success, our foot in the door of fame.

We watched the single gradually climb the charts. When it entered the Top 20 – it peaked at No.15 – we got on *Top Of The Pops* as a hit act. The show was recorded on a Wednesday and went out on a Thursday. We went down to London and were in the BBC studio from 9am to 9pm. We did a couple of rehearsals, then the proper take. That was fantastic. We never were a screamer band – we weren't pretty enough – but the girls loved us because of our rough and ready look. They were singing along and dancing as much as the blokes. We were still seen as skinheads, but we had mellowed our look quite a lot. Our hair was growing down at the back on to our collars, like the skinhead girls and we were wearing colourful clothes instead of the jeans and Ben Sherman shirts.

The next evening, we watched the show together. It wasn't our first time on, but it was our first as a hit band, which made all the difference. I remember thinking, 'That's it! We've made it. We're famous at last. All those years of graft have come to fruition.' Of course, my parents loved it. *Top Of The Pops* was an institution. Every family watched it. My mum phoned me after we had been on. 'All the neighbours have been round to say they saw you on TV.' That was the big buzz for her.

A few weeks later, our spirits were dampened with some news from Chas. 'You're being sued.' We had always thought that 'Get Down and Get With It' was an original Little Richard song. He was given the writer credit on his record. It turned out that it was a bloke called Bobby Marchant who really wrote it. He had done the original version, which we had never heard. The record company sorted out the lawsuit, but we learnt to be more careful in future.

*

'Get Down and Get With It' changed everything for us. It was the start of our mushrooming success. Where we had been struggling before because of our look, suddenly it didn't matter. All we had to worry about was the dreaded follow-up. Chas was insistent that we couldn't put out another cover. 'You have to sit down and write a hit record. If you want to be seen as serious artists, you need an original hit.' He said he knew we could do it, but we weren't so confident.

For the first time, Jimmy and I got together on our own to write. Our previous partnerships hadn't been much of a success, so we had nothing to lose. Jimmy came over to my house and we sat down with our guitars. We didn't have a clue what we were aiming for. We just wanted to write any song. We started off with a riff that we had made up ages ago. We used to play it in the dressing room to tune up his violin. We knew it was catchy, because people who heard it always asked what it was. It was nothing, a practice tune. Twenty minutes later, we had written 'Coz I Luv You'. We put a chord progression over the riff and that was it. We just jammed it and I sang a melody. The words came off the top of my head. Straight away, we knew we had something. It was so different from anything we had written before.

The next day, we took the song to Chas in London. In those days, bands didn't do demos, so we had to sit in his office and play it on our guitars. We weren't nervous because we knew Chas so well, but we were a bit apprehensive about his reaction. Chas was always critical. He didn't pussyfoot around. If he thought something was crap, he would sure as hell tell you. We played it, then mumbled a few words about wanting to put a violin on it to make it more distinctive. Before we'd even finished talking, he said, 'I think you've written your first hit record. In fact. I think you've written your first No.1.' We thought he was joking. He said, 'I'm serious. Do you have anything else?' We didn't. We had only written it the day before, on our first attempt.

Chas insisted we go straight into the studio to record the

track. We had one rehearsal to work out the other parts and the violin solo, but that wasn't a problem because the song was so simple. It was just very instant and straightforward, which we later realised is what a hit record is all about. We cut it in two days. To be honest, we didn't like it that much, although we knew that Chas loved it. We thought it sounded weak next to 'Get Down'. It was catchy, but it was too poppy – not heavy enough to be a Slade song. We suggested to Chas that we try what we had done on 'Get Down' and add some stamping and clapping to fill it out. So we did. We built the track up and up and went out on the violin. I came up with a simple vocal riff that followed the chords near the end and that became another hook. It also became another of our trademarks. It all just fell into place.

All that was wrong with the song after that was the title. Then, it was 'Because I Love You'. 'It looks wet,' I told Chas. 'It doesn't suit the sound or our image.' None of us wanted to follow a song called 'Get Down and Get With It' with 'Because I Love You'. I came up with the idea of spelling it to reflect our dialect. It was how we used to scrawl graffiti on bog walls back in the Midlands. We went through various permutations and ended up with 'Coz I Luv You'. It looked less soppy. It had character. Chas was over the moon. He said, 'I guarantee this will go to No.1.' Two weeks after the release, it was bloody well there. We were over the moon.

In those days, the charts came out on a Tuesday. You'd get a phone call at 10am to tell you your position. I remember being at home and getting the call from Chas. He said, 'You've done it! I told you it was a No.1 record.' It was the best feeling in the world. I thought, 'This is what we've been working for all these years.' Any band who says it doesn't want to be No.1 is lying, especially if it's been going as long as we had by then. We didn't think of it as our first No.1. It was just a No.1 and all the better that it was the first song that Jim and I had written together. We had hit on the right combination. As a team, the pair of us knew how to write a No.1 record. From then on, Jim and I always wrote together.

Every radio station played 'Coz I Luv You' to death. It was a great radio record. It had character. It was a pop tune with a catchy melody. The vocal and the violin in particular made it stand out. It sold half a million copies in two weeks. We were doing press every day. Everyone wanted a piece of us. On the afternoon that we went to No.1, we travelled down to London to do *Top Of The Pops* the next day. We barely said a word to each other. We were too excited to talk. We were going to be on *Top Of The Pops* in the No.1 spot, which was a killer. We had done the show the week before when we were No.2, but this was so much better. We had knocked Rod Stewart's 'Maggie May' off the top spot. That was a classic record. It had been No.1 for weeks and everyone thought it would stay there for ages. All I thought on the way down to London was 'Oh my God, we've knocked Rod Stewart off the top of the charts.' It was unbelievable.

The next day at the *Top Of The Pops* studio, several cases of Champagne arrived from the record company. We had a party in our dressing room to celebrate. I was rat-arsed, inviting all the other bands to join us. It was like that every time we played the show from then on. We virtually became a resident act because of the string of hits we had. At one stage, we were on almost every week. Playing *Top Of The Pops* became like falling off a log. The producer loved us, because we livened the place up. All the different artists and record company people loved us, because we always had drink in our dressing room and it was open house.

Playing *Top Of The Pops* made us realise how different we were from a lot of other bands. We made a point of enjoying ourselves and we never put on a cool image, no matter how big a hit we had. Some acts acted like stars, even backstage. They refused to mingle with the others and their dressing rooms were strictly off limits. We didn't want to be like that. We wanted to have a giggle and meet as many people as possible. Whether we stayed famous or not, we were determined that Slade was going to be good fun for as long as it lasted.

MADE IT MA!
TOP
OF THE CHARTS

6

'Coz I Luv You' topped the charts for three weeks in November 1971. For us, it began a rollercoaster ride which was to last for five years. It was a whirlwind of gigs, radio shows, TV appearances, recording and travel. After all those years of graft, we were suddenly the bee's knees. Everyone wanted a piece of us. Even the teen press loved us. That was weird. Our skinhead image had frightened off younger fans in the past, but having a No.1 record seemed to make all the difference. We had to come to a decision about our image. Lots of girlie magazines wanted to interview us too, but we weren't sure if we wanted to be seen as a pop act.

In the early '70s, there were basically two types of bands – those that sold singles and those that sold albums. The singles bands were pop. Their audiences were made up mainly of girls who went to gigs to scream at their idols. Even The Beatles had more girls than boys at their shows. When I saw The Beatles at Birmingham Hippodrome, after they had made it, I couldn't hear any of the songs for all the screaming. I remember the *NME* used to put on poll winners' concerts at Wembley, which were exactly the same. Album acts were a different kettle of fish. They were much cooler. They played proper gigs at places like The Marquee, where fans went to get into the music and dance. The problem was that as soon as you had a hit, you became a screamer band. The only way to avoid it was to make a conscious effort to steer clear of the teen press and in particular the girlie mags.

As far as Dave and I were concerned, we wanted to be both pop and cool, which was unheard of at the time. Bands were either one or the other, but we didn't see why we couldn't be both. We wanted to sell singles and albums. Don didn't much care how we were perceived, but Jim hated the thought of us being a pop act. It didn't sit easy with him. He thought it undermined our songs. To be honest, I think Jim would rather have been in Led Zeppelin than Slade. He wasn't comfortable with being interviewed or photographed full-stop, never mind talking to someone who wanted to know what he ate for breakfast. In the end, we did do the girlie mags and the teen TV shows. Even Jim accepted that we needed to broaden our appeal, so he gave in, however much he hated it.

Looking back, I think it took a while for our success to sink in. At first, we were more relieved than anything. We were beginning to wonder if we would ever have a hit and knew that the record company felt the same way. In those days, if you signed a five-year deal with a label, you were with them for five years and you were under contract to put out five albums. No-one wanted to be lumbered with a band who didn't have hits and we were wise enough to know that, eventually, Polydor would give up trying with our records.

The biggest change we saw was at the venues. Even after our No.1, we were still doing clubs. We were booked into venues for the next six months and we were determined to fulfil those dates. I guess we could have cancelled them, but we felt bad about letting down the fans and promoters who had supported us when we were struggling. At a few clubs, we got a higher fee because of our success, but most just paid us the same amount of money. The reaction we got was phenomenal. We were turning up at tiny venues to see hundreds of people queuing outside, desperate to get in. Fans just couldn't believe that this big band, who they had seen on *Top Of The Pops* was still playing their little local theatres. It was mayhem.

I remember one gig we did at a country club just outside

of Birmingham. The place is now part of a huge golf club. We had played there loads in the past and we usually sold it out. We had one show still booked there and we told the promoter we'd definitely do it. The venue was right off the road and when we turned up, the queue to get in stretched for half a mile. This was at two in the afternoon. When we went on stage, people were standing outside, trying to watch through the windows. That was probably the first time we realised how insanely popular we had become.

Our next step after 'Coz I Luv You' was to record an album. That put us under a bit of pressure. Not only did it have to be good to maintain our success, but it had to come out as quickly as possible. In the '70s, bands didn't write an album first, then take singles off it. In fact, most of our hits didn't appear on albums until much later. Fortunately, Chas had the answer to our problem. 'I think you should do a live album,' he told us. 'We'll just put on a gig and record it.' That came as a shock. Live albums weren't particularly popular then. As usual though, Chas had thought it all through. For a start, our old fans would love it, because they were already familiar with the songs. It would also be the perfect introduction to Slade for the kids who had just got into us. Even better, it would take no time at all to record.

Chas booked a big studio just off London's Piccadilly Circus for three nights to record the album. We were to play three gigs – from Tuesday to Thursday – then mix and match the best tracks from each one. The place was like a small theatre – it could hold an audience of around 200, but it wasn't a proper venue. We put an announcement out on the radio for people to come down for free and invited members of our fan club.

On the second night, the Wednesday, we went to the studio straight from *Top Of The Pops*. 'Coz I Luv You' was still No.1 and we had made our third or fourth consecutive appearance on the show. As it turned out, every track that ended up on the album was recorded that night. For some reason, all four of us were on a real high. It was just one of those nights that you knew was going to be great. The atmosphere in the studio was electric. It was like throwing a private party. We could have done whatever we wanted on stage and the crowd would have gone crazy. Every single one of them wanted to be heard on the record, so they were shouting even louder than usual. By the time we had finished the first song, they were all really rowdy. That was exactly what we wanted. It spurred us on and we put in a great performance. You can hear it on the album. We were having a fantastic old time.

One of my favourite Slade moments ever happened that night. We were doing a song called 'Darling Be Home Soon', which was originally by John Sebastian. It was basically a quiet ballad that built up into a huge crescendo. Just before the big ending, when we were all playing very softly, I accidentally did a massive burp. I had been drinking all day and I couldn't help it. Of course the crowd dissolved into laughter. Even we thought it was really funny. When we listened back to it afterwards, it sounded brilliant, so we kept it in. It became a trademark of our version of that song. Every time we played it at gigs, I was supposed to recreate this burp. If I didn't do it, people would be disappointed. They thought it was part of the track.

The album was mixed on the Friday, the day after the last show. All in all, it took less than a week to put together. Prior to mixing, the total cost of recording was £400. We decided to call it *Slade Alive* , because that's basically what it was. It captured exactly what we were about and had a real sense of humour. The only thing left to do was decide on the sleeve. Again, that was Chas' idea – well, sort of. 'We're going to get one of the fans to design the sleeve,' he told us. 'We're having a competition and the best entry goes on the cover of the album.' We loved that. Anything that involved the fans was okay with us.

The competition ran a few days later in *The Sun*. There were thousands of entries. We were gobsmacked. Some of them were fabulous. The prize was not only to design the sleeve but to come with us on our first ever trip to America. The paper gave us what they had chosen as the five best entries and asked us to pick our favourite. Typically, we ended up with the most off-the-wall one. It was a cartoon of two teddy bears, one huge and one little, standing side-by-side. It had nothing whatsoever to do with the album – we just loved it. It was a great drawing, very tongue-in-cheek, and it made us laugh. In the end, it didn't actually go on the cover, but on the inside of the gatefold sleeve. We also printed reviews of our shows – good and bad – on the inside, which no bands had ever done before. On the front of the sleeve, we had a picture of us on stage. It was in red and black, just shadows of us really. It was hard to tell it was us at all, unless you looked closely. A couple of years later, a fan turned up in our dressing room at a show and insisted he take off his shirt. He had a tattoo of the cartoon bears, which covered the whole of his back. It was just the outline, but he was going to have it coloured in.

Slade Alive came out in early 1972 and was a huge hit. It went straight to No.1 and stayed in the charts for another eighteen months. It was massive in countries all over the world. Even today, people still tell me that it was their favourite Slade album. It captured the energy of our live shows, but it was commercial. It also helped set us apart from other pop acts. We weren't just a singles band anymore, we had a credible, raunchy hit album too. We were pop and we were cool. It was perfect.

Slade Alive saw us getting further away from our old skin-head image. We had started to wear much more colourful clothes and both Jim and Dave had grown their hair. Our new look didn't frighten the pop fans, which was important. It was also better for us when we went abroad. Venues didn't have to worry about the type of audience we might attract.

The first country we began visiting regularly was Holland. 'Get Down and Get With It' had charted there even before it was a hit in Britain. Then we had gone over to play *Top Pop*, which was the Dutch equivalent of *Top Of The Pops*. That was great for us. It made us popular very quickly. After that, we were invited back to play at a festival in the middle of a park in Amsterdam. When we got there, we found out we were the headline act. It was our first proper festival appearance and we were top of the bill. The venue was great – a huge park with a lake in the middle. There was only one problem. Right in front of the stage was a big tree. Chas hit the roof when he saw it. He was screaming at the promoters, 'My band's not playing behind a bloody tree. Get rid of it or they're not going on.' You have to hand it to Chas – whatever he wanted, he made sure he got. By the time the festival started, someone had chopped down the tree.

On that particular trip to Amsterdam, we were booked into an hotel called the 13 Balken. That was the first time we had stayed there. It was a real nitty-gritty place, smack bang in the centre of the red-light district. It took me back to my days in Frankfurt. We were due to be in Holland for a week and we based ourselves at that hotel the whole time. We had an absolute ball. We'd seen some similar red-light areas in Germany, but we'd never really experienced what they were like. We couldn't believe our eyes. The first day, we walked around just staring at the sex shops. We were amazed at all these women sitting in the windows. We thought it was great.

The next morning, when we went down to breakfast, all the hookers were there having something to eat. We got chatting to them and they told us about their kids and their lives and how they had got into prostitution. After that, every time we went to Amsterdam, we booked into the 13 Balken. We became quite pally with the girls who hung out around there. They had great stories about their clients and what men had asked them to do. It was fascinating for us to chat to them about their kids or whatever in the morning, then see them with their tits out in shop windows at night. When we'd stayed at the hotel a few times, we'd put them on the guest list for our gigs and they'd offer us freebies in return!

The bloke who owned the hotel was a real character. He was mad, totally mad, but we got on great with him. For a while, we went back to the 13 Balken even when we could afford better hotels. Eventually, as we became more popular, we had to stay at bigger places for security reasons. We still saw the owner though. He came to every one of our gigs. During the day, he used to drive his motorbike around the streets of Amsterdam like a lunatic. A couple of years later, he was killed on his bike. No one was surprised. He was an accident waiting to happen, but we loved him for his craziness.

Our trips abroad became more and more frequent. Up until 'Coz I Luv You' came out, we had spent only the odd week abroad, usually in Germany, Holland or Belgium. Suddenly, we had a hit all over Europe, so we had to go to every territory to promote it. We weren't really touring as such. We would go to a country to record a TV show, then play maybe two or three one-off gigs over the next couple of days. By then, we had a proper van and two permanent road crew, although we were still a very small-time operation.

Our next single, 'Look Wot You Dun', came out in February 1972. By then, we were on non-stop promotional tours. It was madness. One day we'd be in Germany, the next in Scandinavia. Mainly, we went to appear on TV shows. Everywhere had their own equivalent of *Top Of The Pops*. They were always popular programmes and they could double your popularity overnight. One of the main shows in Germany was called *Beat Club*. All the big bands of the '60s and '70s appeared on it. It was one of the highest-rating programmes on German TV. Another one was called *Music Laden*. That always had a bizarre mix of European and English acts on. It was like a variety show with two or three rock or pop bands, plus a few traditional German singers.

It was at one *Music Laden* recording that we first bumped

into Abba. They were great fun. We'd do three or four TV shows in one country in the space of a week. It seemed like they were always on the same ones. In the morning, they would be at the airport, waiting to take the same plane as us. It was so funny to see them first thing in the morning, looking all bleary eyed and ragged. They often looked worse than we did. Then we'd watch them recording a show, all perfectly made-up and immaculately dressed. Abba knew who we were, because we had started getting big hits in Scandinavia. We were the pop stars in their eyes; they were the up-and-coming band. They were always really friendly though. A lot of European bands were frightened by our look, particularly the ones who had seen us in our skinhead phase. Most were wary of coming over to talk to us. Abba weren't bothered. Another act we later became big pals with was Boney M. It sounds like the match made in hell – Slade and Boney M – but we had a great time when we got together.

I couldn't say how many telly shows we did over the next few months, but it must have been hundreds. As a band, we were perfect for TV. The Europeans loved us because we were so over the top. Their own acts weren't like that at all. It wasn't hard to look good next to them. Visually, we were fantastic. We'd do whatever it took to make our performance more exciting than everyone else's. We'd kick the drums over or smash our instruments if need be.

Even in the '80s, recording TV shows in Europe wasn't the same as it was in Britain. In Germany, we would perform alongside dozens of other acts. The shows were filmed in huge 10,000-seat-halls. We often spent three days on each one. The first day was a just a rehearsal for the camera and soundmen. For us, it was a complete waste of time. We'd waste most of the day eating and drinking and meeting the other bands. There was nothing else to do. The second day was a dress rehearsal, which an entire audience was brought in to watch. That was a giggle, at least it was for me. On the third day, the show was recorded for real with a new audience. That was three days spent on a three-minute song. It was as much trouble as putting on a gig.

In France, it was different again. They didn't have straightforward pop programmes at all. We went on variety shows with French comedians and dancers. We were stuck in there as the token pop act. Once, we came on after a female contortionist in a glittery leotard. We played alongside a lot of animal acts too – like dogs jumping through burning hoops. It was like a circus show, but on telly. It was a very odd mish-mash. The staff at French TV stations were incredible. They didn't give a toss. They took lunch from midday to 3 or 4pm. All the crew just disappeared. It was chaos. It never seemed like anything was happening, then suddenly lots of people would start running around, shouting.

In the '70s, France was a very strange market for English bands. The country had only one pop radio station, so it took ages for a record to get going there. Songs would build up gradually over months, slowly picking up more and more airplay. When we released 'Merry Xmas Everybody' in 1973, it only just crept into the French charts. By the time it had reached No.1, it was Easter 1974.

Every time we released a record, we went back and did all the same European TV shows. There was no other option. The video market didn't exist, at least not like it does today. We did make promotional films for singles, which were sent out to places like Australia that we couldn't get to, but they were nothing like modern videos. They were just cheap simple short films, with the song stuck on as a soundtrack. We'd usually shoot them running round London. We made one in Euston Station, with the four of us going up and down the escalators. We shot quite a few in recording studios too. We'd sit around with headphones on and pretend we were laying down the track. Videos didn't become a big marketing tool until many years later. Bands didn't bother much about them, because there were very few programmes which would play them. In Britain, local magazine shows on at 6pm might broadcast a clip if we were playing in the area that night or the single was selling particularly well, but that was about it. Pop shows wanted the bands themselves in the studio, either miming or playing live.

Between the TV shows, travel and gigs, we had to find time to write and record new songs. Chas was determined that we would put out one single straight after another. As soon as one dropped out of the charts, we had to have the follow-up ready to go. We literally had non-stop hits for the next four years. There was never more than three or four months between each release, depending on how long the previous single before had stayed in the Top 30. 'Look Wot You Dun' came out three weeks after 'Coz I Luv You' finally fell out of the charts. It went in quite low, then climbed to No.2 over the next month or so. It wasn't the same big success as 'Coz I Luv You', but it was more than enough to keep us in the public eye and keep the album selling well. It was an odd follow-up single, very different from 'Coz I Luv You' and not at all representative of what we were playing on stage. It didn't have the brash sound that had become our trademark. It was just a very simple pop song, written on piano. We knew at the time that it wasn't one of our best records, but we had to put something out straight away. We couldn't go back to releasing covers and 'Look Wot You Dun' was the best we could come up with at such short notice.

In the spring of 1972, we went out on our first proper tour. Had it not been for the club gigs already booked when 'Coz I Luv You' went to No.1, we would have toured earlier. With those out of the way, we could finally start playing big theatres. On our debut tour, we took Status Quo out as our opening act. They were playing the same circuit as us at the time. They had changed their image since the '60s, when they had their first hits. They had become this denim-clad boogie-rock band.

The tour was an instant sell-out. We knew it would be. All our old fans wanted to see us play theatres and a lot of our new fans hadn't been able to get tickets for the smaller shows. We played every major city in Britain. The opening night was in Glasgow at Green's Playhouse, which later became the Apollo. Glasgow was a notoriously hard gig. If the fans liked you, it was great. If they didn't, they had no problem letting you know about it. We had been big in Scotland for years, so we knew we'd go down well. Still, we were shocked at the reaction. We had never experienced anything like it before. The crowd went absolutely mental. We were used to wild audiences, but this was out of control.

I remember being a bit worried before we went on, because the stage in Green's Playhouse was incredibly high. I thought we might feel isolated from the fans because we were used to playing on small club stages with them right in front of us. When we walked on, the place erupted. Fortunately, we had a fantastic sound system. If we hadn't had, I don't think anyone would have heard us, because the noise from the audience was deafening. That was the first time screamer girls had turned up to our shows. The best thing about it was that it wasn't just girls. The audience was half male, half female. We had both the teeny-bop fans and the lads who were into bands like Deep Purple. It was the perfect mix.

That night in Glasgow was the first time we realised we had broken through. It hadn't seemed real to us before. Suddenly, we felt like real pop stars. We were staying in nice hotels and we were surrounded by security. When we had arrived at the hotel that afternoon, there were thousands of kids waiting to see us. It was even worse at the venue. It was the first time we couldn't walk down the street or go out on our own. From that day on, our lives would never be the same again.

After the gig, I almost got arrested. Two men from the sheriff's office turned up in the dressing room as soon as we'd come off stage. They threatened to take me into custody. Apparently, I had said 'fuck' on stage and some kid's parents had complained. I did it regularly. I wasn't trying to be controversial. That was just the way I spoke.

You can imagine Chas when these coppers appeared. The room was packed with people drinking and partying when they walked in wearing their uniforms. The whole place fell silent. At first, everyone thought they were just checking for drugs. Then the pair of them came over to me and asked if I had said the f-word on stage. I said it was probably some-one else. I said, 'Honestly, officers, I wouldn't swear with so many youngsters in the audience.' Chas' face was a picture. He was trying to handle it calmly, but you could tell he was freaking out. It was the last thing he needed on the first night of a sold-out tour. In the end, the coppers were okay about it. They were just trying to teach me a lesson. They had to give me a warning though, because it was part of their job and someone had made a complaint. Besides, it would have been hard to prove. What were they going to do – question 3,000 people? The next day, the story was in all the papers. It wasn't a big scandal or anything. Nothing nasty was written. It was just a silly spacefiller. Had they actually taken me away, it would have been better pub-licity. We had journalists phoning us up for a comment. I think I said it was a gag I had told on stage. It was really nothing worse than kids hear every day at school.

On the night of the gig, after the police had let me go, we all went back to the hotel for a drink. Billy Connolly had been at the gig and he turned up in the bar to meet us. He was a big name as a comedian in Scotland, but he had been a folk singer before that, in a group called the Humblebums with Gerry Rafferty in the late '60s. I had never met him before, but I knew his name from having played Scotland so much. He came over for a chat and said, 'How are you finding the fame? I don't know how you handle all the kids outside.' He was worried about how he would cope when it started happening to him. He said, 'I'm getting recog-nised a lot too. I hate it.' I wasn't sure what to say. It was all new to us too. That was the first night we had to be escorted in and out of the venue by police. I hadn't really got my head around it either. The problem with Billy was that you couldn't easily mistake him for someone else. At the time, he had this huge beard. I told him, 'There's no way you'll be able to disguise yourself. Wherever you go from now on, you're going to be recognised. You'll just have to live with it.' It was exactly the same for us. There was no way out of it. After that night. I knew I'd never have a normal life again. It was the start of a whole different ballgame.

The rest of the tour was fantastic. Our profile went through the roof. We really were the new pop sensations. We were accosted by groups of screaming kids wherever we went. We'd come out of theatres, jump into the back of a police van and be ferried off somewhere. All we saw were hoards of people banging on the sides of the van. We weren't prepared for the madness. When we had played clubs, we'd always had kids waiting at the stage door wanting to meet us, but this was on a different level. We were filling 3,000-capacity indoor venues and there were often that many people again standing outside, who couldn't get in.

Dave, Don and I liked the adulation, but Jim hated it. He never got into the rock'n'roll lifestyle. He liked writing songs and being in the studio, but he wasn't keen on coming into contact with the fans. He hated touring. After the gigs, Jim preferred to go to bed than go out. He slept more than anyone I've ever met. As soon as we got to a city, Jim would say he was tired and go straight to his room. Then he'd soundcheck, play the gig and head back to the hotel. He just didn't like being away from home. Dave was the opposite. He didn't mind being in the studio, but it was the performances that he lived for. He loved being recognised in the street and having to fight off the fans. I liked it at first, but it soon became a pain. Kids would camp outside the hotels chanting all night. I sometimes tried to go out in disguise, with a hat pulled over my face. If I got spotted, it was a nightmare. Dave just strode out into the street in his outrageous gear. He thrived on the attention.

After the tour, we had a lot to live up to. We had sold out big venues in every big city and now we had to top that. It was a strange situation for us to be in. Until then, we had been fighting for success. We suddenly realised that it was going to be just as hard to keep it up as it was to get it in the first place. We were determined not to let it slide. We had to be very careful about what we did next. Bring out the wrong record and it could all be over overnight. We were very conscious of that. We knew the next single had to be a corker.

In June, we released 'Take Me Bak 'Ome'. It was a far better single than 'Look Wot You Dun'. It was classic Slade, really rowdy and boisterous. At first, it didn't have the impact we had hoped. Like 'Look Wot You Dun, it entered the bottom end of the charts and only began to climb very slowly. Then we got a big break. We were invited to play the Lincoln Festival, which was being put on in a vast field in Lincolnshire by the actor Stanley Baker. I don't know why he was involved, except that he was a big music fan. It was a three-day event and the first big festival since the Isle Of Wight. The other acts were all much hipper than us, not your usual pop-singles bands. There was Joe Cocker, The Beach Boys, Rod Stewart and The Faces, Status Quo and Lindisfarne. Apparently, we were only asked to be on the bill because Stanley Baker was a Slade fan.

The festival ran from Saturday through to Monday. It was a May bank-holiday. We were to play on the Sunday, the day that The Beach Boys were headlining. Our slot was in the early evening. It had been pissing down with rain the whole of Saturday and all Sunday morning and afternoon. The audience was drenched and the ground was all muddy. It was a very strange atmosphere. When we arrived at the site, we realised that we were due to come on straight after Monty Python's Flying Circus. We thought that was a terrible slot. Monty Python was too weird an act for us to follow. In fact, it turned out to be perfect. We later discovered that Chas had really pushed for us to go on then. It was just as well he didn't tell us that at the time. We would have killed him. Chas had worked out that this slot would have us going on stage at exactly twilight, when the sun was setting. It would be the first time all day that the crowd would be able to see the stage lights. Chas thought it was important for us to be properly lit because we were a lot more visual than the other bands.

We got booed when we walked on stage that evening. It was the first time that had ever happened to us. The audience was incredibly hip and they hated pop bands, which most of them thought we were. Just the fact that we had had a No.1 hit was enough to put them off us. It wasn't the whole crowd who booed, but it was enough people to disconcert us. We carried on regardless. There was nothing else to do. As luck would have it, two minutes into our set, the rain went off. Then all the lights came on. Suddenly, the whole audience stood up. They had been sitting down all day.

After the first song, people began going berserk. The place just exploded. We took everyone by surprise, particularly the press. We could see them down the front, ready to slag us off. Even they were on their feet, dancing. We knew we had taken the place by storm. It was a fantastic feeling. We were only allowed one encore, but we could have played on for hours. When we finally came off stage, the crowd was still going mad. They were chanting for us to return. We weren't sure what to do. We looked at the organisers and they were just waving us on to go back out.

My mind was racing about what we should do for a second encore. We had nothing planned. Then I saw Stanley Baker standing with Chas at the side of the stage. Both of them were beaming. Suddenly, a mad idea popped into my head. I went up to the microphone and thanked Stanley for putting on the festival and invited him to come on and take a bow. As he was walking on, I started doing the Zulu chant, from the film *Zulu* that he had starred in. The rest of the band joined in, then the entire audience. Stanley absolutely loved it. It was the perfect end to our set.

The next week, we were on the cover of every music paper in the country. During the show, I had worn a big bowler hat. The reviews all said that I had looked like a character from *Clockwork Orange*. I hadn't thought of that. I just liked the hat. I had stuck a badge on the front. It was upside down, but it read, 'The Pope smokes dope'. There were photos of me on all the front pages, with my arms raised above my head and the bowler hat on. The impact of that gig was amazing. We broke into a new market overnight. We were up there with all these monster-name credible bands. The sales of 'Take Me Bak 'Ome' went crazy after that. The following week, it was No.1.

Thanks to Chas insisting that we put out a new single every few months, we were having non-stop hits. It was a standing joke that we were the house-band on *Top Of The Pops*. We were often on four or five weeks in a row. In those days, it wasn't a big deal for a song to stay at No.1 for a month. But our constant TV appearances did present us with a problem. We were so well-known for our outfits, that we had to come up with a different look every time we were on. That was what drove us to wear madder and madder gear. Dave and I were the most extreme, although Dave was always more outrageous than me. Dressing up was his big thing. He had most of his clothes made by a lad in the Midlands called Steve. The pair of them used to consult on what look to go for next. It was a weekly ritual.

At *Top Of The Pops*, Dave would never change in front of us. We'd all be in the dressing room getting ready and he would disappear off to the bog. He didn't want us to see him putting his outfit on gradually. He would only appear when he had the lot on. It was the full effect or nothing. Every week, the whole band, plus Chas and some guys from the record company, would sit and wait for Dave to come out of the toilet in whatever he was wearing for the show. We'd have had a few drinks by then and things had always started to get silly. We'd seen his outfit coming in in its covers and hanging up on a rail, but you could never tell exactly what it was like until he had it on. I used to say 'Come on out, Dave. Reveal all.' It was ridiculous. He'd make this big entrance, then stand there waiting for our comments.

▲ *Just checking everything is in order –*
aged 9 months

▲ *Who's a pretty boy then? On holiday in*
Rhyl aged 2.

▶ *Aged 11 with my*
first guitar, practising
chords. The budgie was
not impressed.

▲ *The Phantoms on stage at the Three Men in a Boat.*

▲ *The Memphis Cutouts, rhythm and blues combo extraordinaire!*
Left to right: Gerry, Terry, Phil, Me and Pete.

► *Typical early '60s handout shot. Steve Brett and the Mavericks.*

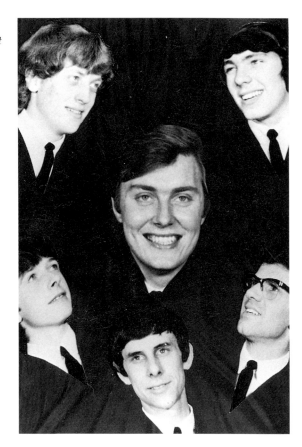

▼ *The 'N Betweens on return from the Bahamas. The name change to Ambrose Slade not far away.*

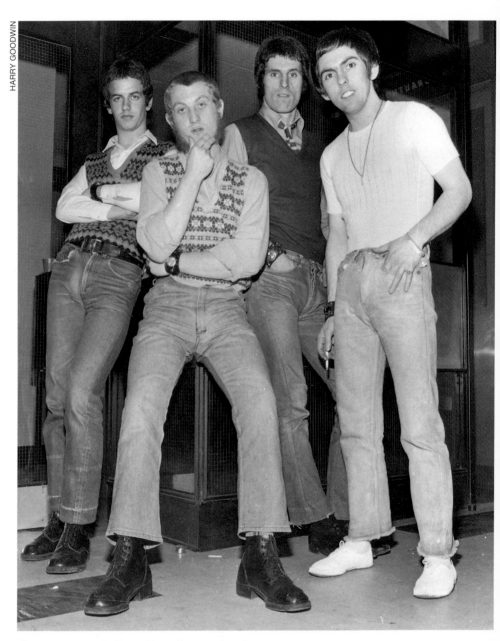

HARRY GOODWIN

▲ *The NEW LOOK! Would you let your daughter date these boys!? Slade are launched.*

▶ *Chas Chandler the mentor, bass player with The Animals and producer and manager of Jimi Hendrix and Slade.*

HARRY GOODWIN

▼ *Dad Jack and mum Leah, happy but still thinking "When's he going to get a proper job?"*

HARRY GOODWIN

▲ *Pensive, puckering pop star!*
My girlfriend Suzan's favourite pin-up.

▲ *Slade – the epitome of sartorial elegance!*

GERED MANKOWITZ

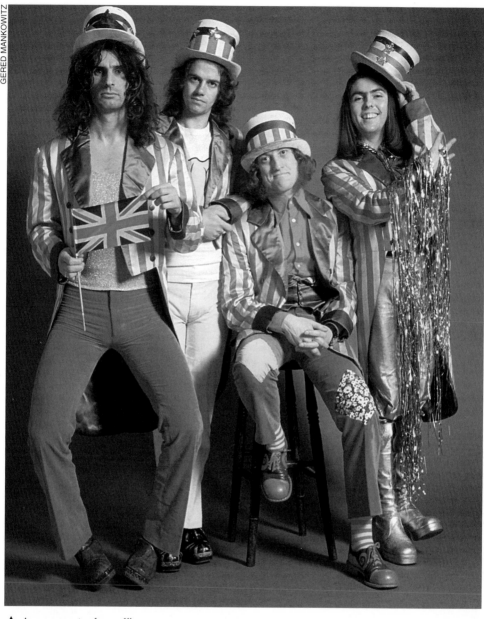

▲ *Any excuse to show off!*

REX FEATURES

▲ *Pose 42 from the Rock 'n' Roll handbook.*

REX FEATURES

▲ *Another day, another TV show, but who knows where..? We just kept on rocking.*

HARRY GOODWIN

◀ *This is what
you call a tie!*

GERED MANKOWITZ

▲ *Publicity shot from Slade's big screen debut –* Slade in Flame.

REDFERNS/MICHAEL OCHS ARCHIVES

▲ *Slade in '76. The American sojourn.*

REX FEATURES

▲ *Slade on stage in the early '80s.*

▶ *Vic Reeves and Bob Mortimer as Noddy and Dave, living entirely on Cup-A-Soups.*

BBC TELEVISION

JOHN BROWN PUBLISHING

MIRABELLE SUNSHINE POP BOOK DECEMBER 1974

◀ Immortalised in Viz magazine.

▲ Slade get the teen mag treatment.

◄ *My flabber was ghasted! Michael Aspel catches me with the big red book on* This is Your Life.

▼ *That's my boy. Me and Django.*

▶ *Daddy's girls! Charisse and Jessica at my 50th birthday party.*

▼ *The three teachers from* The Grimleys *TV comedy–drama series. Me as music teacher Mr Holder, with Amanda Holden as Miss Titley and Brian Conley as Doug Digby.*

GRANADA TELEVISION

ANDREW JOHN PHOTOGRAPHY

▲ *Look to the future now, it's only just begun...*

Dave did wear the most unbelievable clothes. Of course, the audience thought he was bonkers. What they probably didn't realise was that we thought exactly the same. Once, he walked out of the bog in a suit that was covered head-to-toe in feathers. We used to give all his outfits nicknames. That one was Foghorn Leghorn, like the cartoon cockerel, the one that went 'I said, I said . . .'. One of his most over-the-top outfits was a long black robe, which he'd wear with a headdress that looked like a Cleopatra wig. The head-dress was metal and silver, shaped just like his own haircut. We called that one The Metal Nun. We took the piss out of him something rotten, but Dave didn't care. He was impossible to insult. All the other bands would take one look at him and fall about laughing, but it went straight over Dave's head. To be fair, it was great for TV. It drove the kids in the studio wild. You could see them staring at him, thinking, 'Who is this headcase? Who would have the audacity to wear such an outfit in front of millions of people?'. I mean, I was bad enough. I had no room to talk. But Dave always had to go that one step further.

Jim couldn't stand Dave's clothes. He thought they were turning the band into a joke. He'd say, 'We don't need all this flash stuff. We should let the music do the talking.' The expressions on Jim's face when Dave appeared in his crazy outfits were priceless. He'd beg Dave to change. 'Oh no, H, please . . . You can't wear that.' Dave had this brilliant line which he used whenever Jim moaned at him. He'd say, 'You write 'em, Jim. I'll sell 'em.' It was a classic.

By early 1972, we were famous for our platform shoes. We first wore them on *Top Of The Pops* when 'Coz I Luv You' was at No.1. No other bands were wearing them then. Very few people had ever even seen a pair of platforms. Dave and I came across them purely by accident when we were shopping one day in Kensington Market. That was where we used to get loads of our stage gear. It was a real treasure trove of the most outrageous clothes. Freddie Mercury had a stall in there. That was where we first met him. We used to see him all the time and we bought quite a lot of stuff from him. He sold mainly flowery hippy shirts. They weren't really our style, but we always paid him a visit anyway, because we liked him so much. He obviously knew who we were, because we were on telly all the time by then. He used to say to us, 'I'm going to be a famous pop star one day. I'm going to be bigger than you guys.' We were like, 'Fuck off, Freddy, you poser.' He was still Freddy Bulsara in those days. Queen hadn't formed yet and I'm not even sure he was in another band, but he certainly said he was a singer. He hadn't yet come out of the closet, but he was certainly very camp.

Anyway, it was on one of our regular trips to Kenny Market that we came across platforms for the first time. We had never seen anything like them before, not even on kids in the street, never mind on other musicians. I bought a red and yellow pair, which were two platforms high. Dave bought some silver ones, but his were boots rather than shoes and they were much higher. Dave adored them because he was so small. Suddenly, he was the same height as everyone else. As the years went on, his boots got higher and higher. Eventually, he was up to six platforms. It was when Gary Glitter came along that Dave went really over the top. I think the pair of them were in some sort of competition to see who could go the highest.

When we started wearing platforms, glam rock didn't exist. At least, the term 'glam rock' hadn't been invented. I think it first appeared towards the end of 1972, but it was inspired by Marc Bolan, not us. Bolan was our big rival, our only 'glam' contemporary. He had his first big hit with T.Rex about eight months before we broke through. It was 'Ride A White Swan' . I can remember exactly where I was when I heard that song for the first time. We had been playing an all-nighter at The Temple in Wardour Street and we came off stage at about 5.30am. There was a DJ on while we were packing up our gear. Until then, Bolan had been making quite hippyish music. As soon as I heard 'Ride A White Swan', I thought, 'Bloody hell, who is this.' It was a crazy record, but it sounded superb. I went straight up to the DJ and asked who the track was by. I couldn't believe it when he said it was T.Rex.

When glam rock started, it had nothing to do with platform shoes. Visually, it was all about glitter. Bolan kicked it off by sticking some little sparkly tears on his cheeks. Then he began getting into glittery clothes. He never wore platform shoes though, certainly not in the early days. He wore little women's shoes with a strap across the top and a buckle. When Dave first saw Bolan's tears, he flipped out. He thought they were fantastic. You could tell he wished he'd thought of the idea himself. The fact that Bolan got there first didn't stop Dave though. Of course, he had to go overboard with it. Whatever Bolan could do, Dave could do bigger and better. That was how he thought. He covered his face with glitter, he put it in his hair, he had strands of it dangling from his clothes. He loved anything silver. Dave was the glitter man of our band. The rest of us didn't bother with it much. For a while, Jimmy got into wearing sort of sparkly jackets on stage, but it was never my thing. Throughout the whole era, I didn't wear one glittery outfit.

I would describe my image in the glam days as a colourful jack-the-lad. I was basically a spiv. I generally wore big bold checked suits, which I had made by tailors in all different colours and styles. I was the first to start the trend for cut-off trousers. Years later, The Bay City Rollers admitted that they pinched their look from me – the cut-offs and the tartan. I still wore the skinhead braces and sometimes even the bovver boots, but I probably preferred my platforms. I went through a stage of wearing big ties too. I had one with a pattern of blue and white diamonds, that was ridiculously huge. It was really wide and it literally reached down to the ground. I had to be careful not to trip over it.

The only item of clothing I had that you could almost describe as glittery was my famous top hat. Hats always suited me. The big flat cap that I wore on the cover of *Play It Loud* was my trademark between our skinhead phase and glam rock. In the early '70s, that was replaced by my top hat with mirrors. It became a Slade mascot. It was the one thing we were always associated with. I invented it myself. I actually got the idea from Lulu. I was watching her on telly one day, when she performed in a spangly dress. It was reflecting the studio lights and there were little silver flashes coming off it. I thought, 'Bloody hell, that looks fantastic.' I reckoned that if I could do something similar, but make it more intense, it wouldn't only look great on telly, it would work on stage too. I thought about it for a while and came up with the idea of using mirrors. I was inspired by the big mirrorballs you used to get in '70s discos. Basically, what I needed was a mirrorball that I could wear.

What I ended up using were those little round plastic mirrors that hang down on strings in shop-window displays. The question was where to put them on my body. The best place would be somewhere I could move them around and have control of them. My head was perfect for that and hats were my thing anyway. For some reason, I decided that I had to put them on a top hat. I had worn top hats before – I used to team them with long flowing coats when I was in the 'N Betweens. The problem was that top hats have sloping sides and the mirrors wouldn't stick to them. I needed a top hat with straight surfaces. I looked for one for weeks, but I couldn't find one. I didn't even know if they existed, so I tried to get one specially made, but with no success.

One day, Dave and I were in Kensington Market, looking for new platform shoes, when I came across this coachman's hat purely by accident. It was an antique and it was exactly what I had been looking for. It was wide at the bottom and instead of going out at the top, it narrowed in. It was actually called a stove-pipe hat and it was what the drivers of stagecoaches used to wear. I only paid a few quid for it because it was really battered, but that didn't matter. It was still in good enough nick to use. I took it home that night and stuck the mirrors on myself. I put them all round the sides and across the top. It had to be fate, because they fitted on perfectly. There were no gaps at all. When I'd finished, it was just a mass of mirrors.

When I wore the hat on TV, it looked quite good, but you could only see the odd glimpse of light coming off it. On stage, it had a much better effect. I knew that would be the case, but I never imagined just how much it was going to freak people out. I used to wear it at the start of every show. It was very hot and heavy, so I couldn't have kept it on all night – I usually only wore it for the first three numbers. During the third song, I'd stand at the microphone and sing a little quiet bit, then we'd black out the whole stage and the hall. A single spotlight would hit my hat and these huge beams of light would come shooting off it. It looked like I had hit a switch and torches were coming out of my head.

If you only saw the hat on TV, you had no idea how impressive it could be. It was impossible to recreate the effect in a studio. You would have had to black the whole set out and that would never happen. On stage though, it was unbelievable. I could see in the eyes of the audience, when the lights came back on, how amazing it had looked. It was like a mirrorball, but much brighter and I could move it around. I could pinpoint people in the crowd and light them up. I only did that for fifty or sixty seconds of the show, but the hat instantly became a glam-rock icon. It was famous in its own right. These days, people think I wore it for the whole glam era, but I didn't. I think I only used it on two or three world tours. In later years, fans would come up to me after a show and ask why I hadn't worn my hat. They thought I didn't do a gig without it. Abroad, it floored people too. No one ever knew how it was done. They thought it was some sort of sophisticated lighting trick, but really it was the simplest idea.

Over the next couple of years, glam rock exploded. It just got bigger and bigger. It seemed like every month, more and more glam bands would appear on the scene. A lot of them copied our look, but tried to make it even more outrageous. There was no point in it otherwise. Naturally, it just egged Dave on. Visually, he had to top them all. It became a never-ending spiral. They'd try to be more ridiculous than Dave, then he'd have to go one better. It was out of control. Everyone was trying to be the most outrageous. That was what eventually killed glam rock. It got so over the top that you couldn't take it any further.

Musically, it was the same story. As soon as other bands saw glam working for us, they decided to adopt the sound themselves. Every record label was desperate to sign a version of Slade. For a while, it was only us and Bolan. Together, we were at the forefront of the scene. Sweet had already had a few hits, but they weren't a glam act at the time. When they started out, they made bubblegum pop music. The press invented the term glam rock when Sweet changed their sound and Gary Glitter came along. From then on, we were all made out to be alike. That was rubbish. Both Bolan and us had our own very different sounds. He was the pretty boy, quite effeminate. We were more rough and ready. Women loved Bolan. We had female fans, but we were always more of a lads' band. Generally, if you liked one of us, you didn't like the other.

I always thought it was a combination of my voice and the the way our records were made that set us apart from our glam-rock rivals. We were never as studio-produced as other bands. All the Chinn & Chapman acts, like Sweet, Suzi Quatro and Mud, were very cleverly made. They were very pop. Bolan was too, although he was produced by Tony Visconti. No one captured our rowdy sound. Our records were a barrage of noise. It was impossible to pinpoint specific sounds, because Chas rolled them all into one. He used a lot of what he had learned with Hendrix on us. He liked distortion rather than clean edges, which suited our songs. In the studio, we turned everything up as far as we could. We wanted to get as close as possible to the way we were on stage. Together with our big chorus chants, that gave us our own niche. Even when other bands stole some of our ideas, they couldn't copy us. They could emulate us, but never copy us.

Until we came along, no one made rowdy records. No one sang like I did either. I developed that screaming/singing style. When you heard one of our records on the radio, there was no doubt about who it was. I know that Chinn and Chapman were very influenced by us. They were two British songwriters/producers who were hugely successful in the glam rock days. They had already written quite a few hits for Sweet, like 'Little Willy' and 'Wig-Wam Bam', but they were very lightweight pop. As soon as we became successful, they began writing much rowdier material for all their acts. The first rowdy song they wrote for Sweet was 'Blockbuster', which was their biggest ever hit. It was No.1 for a month in early 1973. They did the same with Mud and Suzi Quatro. They wrote 'Can The Can' for Suzi, which was No.1 all over the world.

Gary Glitter was someone else who was into our music. 'Rock and Roll, Part Two', his first hit, was nothing like the records he had been making before. It had a big chant chorus, heavy drums and loud guitars. Gary started singing like me too, in that half-shouting way. Funnily enough, no one even tried to be like Bolan. He was very much out on his own. He had a rocky sound, but his vocals were very laid back. He made great rock'n'roll records with big guitar riffs, but they didn't have the brash crash and bang sound we were known for.

We used to meet Bolan a lot at *Top Of The Pops*. He was tiny, about the same size as Dave, except Dave always looked like he was taller because of his platforms. Bolan was a little skinny bloke with corkscrew hair, very sweet and unassuming. I think we liked each other. At least, I know we all liked him. He was always nice and polite when we met, but it was obvious that he was quite frightened of us. He was very careful what he said to us. He came from a completely different background and you could tell he thought we were a bunch of yobbos from up north. There was definitely a professional rivalry between us though, but it was never as bad as the press made out. We were both massive at the same time. Bolan had broken through before us and he was always our main rival. We caught up with him very quickly in terms of sales and success, then over-took him, which he didn't expect. Bolan didn't have anything like the amount of No.1s we had. For a while though, we were at exactly the same level, both vying for the top spot every week. We were by far the two biggest bands in Britain at the time.

I remember when Bolan came back from his first trip to the States. He went out there a bit before us and he brought back a soul record he had heard on the radio. It was a Betty Wright song called 'Clean Up Woman'. It was a Top 10 hit in the States, but I don't think it ever came out here. He said, 'Noddy, I bought this record for you, because I know you love soul music. I think Slade should do a cover version of it. It's perfect for your voice.' By then, we had started writing our own stuff and Chas didn't want us to do any more covers, but he was right, it would have been great for us. It's still one of my favourite ever records.

My best Bolan story happened in 1972, just after a *Top Of The Pops* recording. With our first big royalty cheques, we had all gone out and bought flash cars. Don had a huge white Bentley. It was identical to one that Bolan had. That day, all four of us had travelled to the *Top Of The Pops* studio in White City in Don's car. Bolan had arrived in his too. They were both parked by the entrance, side by side. By the time we were leaving, thousands of our fans and Bolan's had turned up. In those days, there were no private car parks for bands to get in and out of their cars safely. You had to run through all the fans. I remember there were hundreds of screaming girls waiting for Bolan, and loads of yobbos waiting for us. It was like a crazed mob.

Neither us nor Bolan had bodyguards with us, so we stood at the door for a few minutes, getting ready to make a run for it. Dave and I charged forward together, pushed our way through all these frenzied people, then jumped into the Bentley, shut the doors and locked them. Unbe-known to us, we had jumped into Bolan's Bentley. In all the madness, we hadn't seen Jim and Don and our driver get into the other car. Bolan had been right behind us. Now he was stuck outside, with birds ripping his clothes to shreds and pulling his hair. We were just sat there, breathing a sigh of relief, when we looked behind us and saw the others in Don's car. Then we saw Bolan, just this tiny little elf being attacked by a mob. His jacket had been torn off and his hair was all over the place. Girls were just jumping on him. We had locked him out of his own motor.

The five of us laughed about it later. He knew we didn't do it on purpose. We got on well with him, although we were never big mates. We certainly didn't see each other socially. There was a bit of bickering between us. We'd say, 'Oh, we're No.1 this week, what number are you?', but always in a friendly way. It was really only Dave who felt he was competing with Bolan all the time, but that had more to do with girls and clothes than music.

It wasn't until almost halfway through 1972 that we began to make any money from Slade. The royalties from the singles and the live album had only just started to come in. Until then, we had been living almost a double life. We were these huge stars, having non-stop hits, with our faces on the front of lots of magazines, but we were still pretty poor. Officially, we were all still living in the Midlands, but we very rarely went home. In London, we stayed mainly in a hotel called The Grantley in Shepherds Bush. It was a real rock'n'roll hotel. Loads of bands stayed there. When we first moved in, the four of us had to share the same room. We were still waiting for our profits from the hits. Our gig money hadn't gone up much either. Although we were on much higher fees, we were constantly shelling out for better equipment, more crew and bigger vans. Our outgoings had increased a lot more than our income. Fortunately, we were very sensible about money, which had a lot to do with Chas. He made sure that Slade was always a self-sufficient unit. We never took an advance from the record label, at least not until much later in our career. We had a deal whereby we were signed to Chas' production company and he was signed to the label. We always worked within our means and that stood us in good stead in later years. We were never paying back money, so everything we earned was profit.

The best thing about our financial situation was that, when we did get cheques, we could spend them however we liked. I always said that as soon as I made any money, I was going to buy a Mercedes sports car. So that's what I did. I got it with my first decent royalty cheque. This was about six months after 'Coz I Luv You' had been a hit. I had been in love with Mercedes sports cars since I was a kid. Whenever I'd seen someone in one, I'd said to myself, 'That'll be me one day.' I thought they were real jack-the-lad cars. I bought mine in the Midlands. It was £5,000, which was a lot of money then. I had received a cheque for about £20,000, so suddenly it didn't seem much to me. That was the first real money I ever had. I couldn't believe it when the cheque arrived.

My first Mercedes was light metallic blue. I used to keep it at my parents' place, because I didn't have my own house. You can imagine their reaction when I turned up in it – a Mercedes parked on a working-class council estate – it looked ridiculous. It was surreal for my parents. I don't think they realised how much money I was starting to make. I certainly didn't tell them how much it had cost. That would have frightened them. I knew what they'd say: 'Neville, what were you thinking? You could have bought a small house for that!'

All four of us got cars at the same time. Don had his Bentley and both Dave and Jim bought Rolls-Royces. We already had a Rolls-Royce as a band car. It was a huge black limousine, in which we all travelled together to gigs. We got it mainly for safety reasons. We were being mobbed all the time and getting in and out of theatres was a nightmare. Fans would be jumping on top of the car and clinging to the bonnet. The Rolls-Royce limo was built like a tank, so there wasn't ever much damage done to it and we felt reasonably safe inside. It was Chas who insisted that we buy it. Had it been left to us, we would still have been travelling in a scraggy old van. Chas was having none of that. He said, 'You're the biggest pop stars in the country. You can't be arriving at places in a van.' As soon as we got it, of course, we loved it. It made us feel like stars.

Dave's own Rolls-Royce was silver. He bought it to go with his clothes. Later on, he had it resprayed cream and brown, which looked fantastic. Dave always had a flash car, even before we made it. The band would be skint, but Dave would still manage to keep a sports car. With his dad being a mechanic, he got good deals and all his repairs done for free. When I first met him, he had a Triumph Spitfire. Then he got a Sunbeam Alpine, which had the number plate YOB 1. He kept that plate for many many years. He'd move it from car to car. He even put it on his Rolls-Royce.

Jim was the first out of all of us to buy a house. He got it pretty much straight away, probably with the rest of the money that he hadn't spent on his car. He was always a real home-lover. He liked to be settled in one place. He also had a steady girlfriend, Louise, who had been going out with him since school. She was the only girlfriend he ever had and they're still together today. They got married in the middle of 1972. Jim didn't even tell us he was planning to get married. At least, he didn't tell me. We had a few days off and I was on one of my rare trips home. I nipped out to the shops to get a few things and bought an evening paper. I didn't look at it until I got home. Splashed right across the front page was a photo of Jim and Louise. I think it was taken outside a registry office. I couldn't believe my eyes. He never told me why he had kept it quiet and I never asked him. I said congratulations to Jim the next time I saw him, but it was never mentioned again.

LETTING

LOOSE

IN L.A.

7

After 'Coz I Luv You' and 'Take Me Bak 'Ome' had both gone to No.1, it was a lot harder for us to make an impact. When a new band gets to the top of the charts, it seems fresh and exciting. When you've already been there a couple of times, people don't take as much notice. As usual, Chas had the answer. He said, 'Your next single has to enter the charts really high up, maybe at No.1.' Today, it means nothing for a record to go in at No.1, but back then it was a really big deal. Only five records since the start of the charts in 1952 had gone straight in at No.1.

Chas and John Fruin, the head of Polydor, devised a plan. It was a totally new idea. The pair of them came up with a marketing campaign whereby our single would be played on TV and radio for a few weeks before it was in the shops. Again, it's common practice now, but in the '70s, all bands would cut a single in two days tops, mix it the following day, then it would be pressed, packaged and out the next week. The total turnaround time was about a fortnight. Singles were churned out. No one made an album, then took tracks off it. As soon as you wrote a song that sounded like a single, you'd go into the studio, record it and release it. The albums came later.

Our new single was to be 'Mama Weer All Crazee Now'. I came up with the title after one of our shows. Wherever we played, the venue would be devastated by the end of the night. Loads of seats were always ripped out and smashed to pieces. Our repair bills were astronomical. We never made any money from touring because of it. At the height

of the mayhem, it cost us a fortune. After one particular gig
at Wembley Arena, I walked back out on stage to take a
look at the hall. We had done two shows there that day, one
in the afternoon and another in the evening. They were
both for charity. All the money made was going to build a
new wing on a handicapped kids' school in London, which
we later went to open. All the fans had gone home and the
place was deserted. I looked out at this huge hall and there
was nothing but a massive pile of chairs in the middle of the
floor. The cleaners had chucked them in a heap like it was a
big bonfire. I thought, 'Christ, everyone must have been
crazy tonight!'

Crazy was one of my catchwords on stage. I used to
shout, 'Everybody's crazy,' at the audience between songs,
when they were going really wild. I came up with a song
title there and then. It was 'My my, We're All Crazee Now'.
A couple of days later, Jimmy and I had finished the song
and we played it to Chas on acoustic guitars in the studio.
He said, 'It's brilliant. I love it. And what a great title –
"Mama We're All Crazee Now". What the hell does that
mean?' I said, 'No, no. It's not "Mama", its "My my". . .' As
soon as the words came out of my mouth, I knew 'Mama'
was much better. So, really, it was Chas' idea, although it
was an accident. He had just misheard it.

We all knew 'Mama' was a great single. We had hit on
our benchmark sound. It was perfect for Slade, very
raucous, but catchy and pop. It was a better stage song than
'Coz I Luv You'. It was a real powerhouse record. It had all
the right ingredients, including a long playout at the end
with me singing, 'Mama, mama, mama, mama, yeah!' It
was my ad-libbing again. Chas was fantastic for catching
things like that in the studio. I've never found another
producer who does it. He'd let me sing whatever came into
my head on the spur of the moment, then keep most of it in.
He loved ad-libs. I'd just be trying stuff out and he'd tape
the lot. He never wiped anything. He kept the howl at the
start of 'Mama', which was actually me warming up my
voice. On 'Cum On Feel The Noize', when I go 'Baby, baby,

baby' at the beginning, it was just something I did on a guide vocal to bring the band in. It was never originally intended to be on the record.

Chas' idea of producing was to make the vocal the focal point of the record. Being the singer, I agreed with him, of course. I don't think the others did. Chas used to say, 'The Beatles always based their songs around vocals. You don't plonk a vocal on top of a tune. You build the whole track around it.' That was what made our records so good for radio. My voice always stood out a mile. Chas was also a great one for spontaneity in the studio. I often recorded vocals live with the band playing, just as a run-through. Then that would be the version we'd put out as a single. That happened with 'Get Down and Get With It' and 'Coz I Luv You'. We might have patched bits up here and there, but basically it was us playing live.

Musically, 'Mama' took us to another level. It was a classic Slade song. Everyone loved it and everyone knew all the words. The playout at the end was famous in itself. It went on for a minute after the song finished. On stage, I would sing it to the audience and they'd chant it back. It became another trademark.

As soon as 'Mama' was recorded, Chas put his marketing campaign into action. He got us on *Top Of The Pops* to preview the song and he got us pre-release radio play. Unfortunately, things didn't quite go according to plan. Before the record actually came out, we had to leave for the States. That meant we weren't around during the week of release to do any TV or press interviews. 'Mama' still entered the charts at No.2. The following week, it was No.1. The whole business was flabbergasted. In those days, most records went in at No.30, climbed to No.25, then four or five weeks later got to No.1. Chas said, 'If you can make it to No.2 when you're not even in the country, you can definitely go straight in at No.1 next time'.

By the autumn of 1972, we were starting to get a sniff of radio play in the States. We had been releasing records there since day one. Even our Ambrose Slade album, *Beginnings*, had come out there, although with the title changed to *Ballzy*. I have no idea what was wrong with *Beginnings*. No one ever explained it to us. The cover was totally different too. It had two big balls on it. I don't think *Play It Loud* got an American release, but *Slade Alive* definitely did. It wasn't a big hit, but it caused some waves. It had also got us quite a bit of press and it had done really well in Canada.

'Coz I Luv You' and 'Take Me Bak 'Ome' had both been played a lot by a few big radio stations in the States and Polydor wanted us to go out there to do some promotion. Apart from the fact that we were going to miss the release of 'Mama', it was a good time for us to go. We had just finished the 'Take Me Bak 'Ome' tour and done a European tour. But we were determined not to disappear off to America and ignore our British fans. A lot of bands went over there for twelve months. We couldn't afford to do that. We were riding the crest of our career in both Britain and Europe. Plus, we were very much a singles-orientated act, so our fans expected to see us on *Top Of The Pops* at least every couple of weeks.

Our first US tour lasted less than a month. We could hardly scratch the surface in that time. It wasn't nearly long enough to work the place properly. That was one of our downfalls there. We didn't go out enough in the early days. Still, the experience was a big eye-opener for us. None of us had ever been to the States before. We had got a bit of an inkling of what Americans were like when we played in the Bahamas, but we didn't realise how different they really were. Another thing we hadn't realised was how little we meant over there. We had grown used to the adulation we got from fans at home whenever we walked on stage. In the States, the name Slade didn't mean dick-shit. A few people may have heard of us, but we had no real following whatsoever.

Another mistake we made was to arrive with all guns blazing. Before we had so much as stepped on American soil, we were being hailed as the new Beatles. That was our record company's pre-publicity angle and, ultimately, it didn't work in our favour. The Yanks don't like bands being pushed down their throats. They prefer to discover new acts for themselves. We had an American manager called Peter Kauf and he advised us to come in through the back door without too much fuss. He wanted us to begin by playing little clubs, but Chas wanted us to look like we were stars right from the off. Peter Kauf tried to give Chas advice, but Chas was so single-minded. Nothing would sway him when he had made up his mind. Chas insisted we go in on a high. As for us, we didn't want to be seen as the new Beatles. When the British press had said that about us, we had always replied, 'We're not the new Beatles, we're the first Slade'. That was our stock line. Over there, we couldn't get away with that.

In Chas' defence, he did set us up with some great people. Besides Peter Kauf, who was a very well-known American manager, he got us an agent called Frank Barcelona. Frank was a monster name in the States. He had worked with Chas for years, first with The Animals, then with Hendrix. He was a real high-powered bloke, who carried incredible clout in the business. It was amazing how many important people Chas still knew in America. He probably had even more contacts over there than he did in Britain.

We went straight to the States from the last date of a European tour. Our plane landed in LA. That was crazy land for us. We had never been anywhere like it in our lives. The Yanks must have known it too. We gave ourselves away the moment we arrived. We had got off the plane and collected our luggage. All the Polydor Records people were outside waiting for us. At the time, Polydor wasn't a big label in the States. They had James Brown and James Last, but no big rock or pop acts. We were a real challenge for them and they were determined to do their damnest to get us off the ground there.

We walked out of the airport into blazing sunshine. Talk

about four hicks from Wolverhampton. . . There were two huge black limos waiting for us outside. There was also a big minibus. The limos were for us four band members – two in each. The minibus was for all the road crew we had brought with us. What did we do? Only pile into the minibus! We didn't for a minute think that the limos were for us. The crew loaded all the cases in the back of the bus, we climbed in the front, slammed the doors and the driver was off. By the time the Polydor people realised what was happening, it was too late. They were just stood there, waving their arms and screaming, 'Stop! Don't go in that.' Our roadies couldn't believe their luck. They were left with the limos. They cruised into LA in style. We went in a bloody bus. That was our first foot on American soil. The record company people couldn't believe it. The new Beatles – in a bus!

We were taken to The Hyatt Hotel on Sunset Strip, which was where all the big bands stayed in those days. It was a really famous rock'n'roll hotel. Its full name was The Hyatt House Hotel, but it was known as The Riot House Hotel. It was where Led Zeppelin rode motorbikes up and down the corridors. The place was chaos. All the American groupies hung out there, waiting for whatever new English band was due to arrive. We had never experienced anything like it.

As soon as we walked through the door, there were literally dozens of girls jumping on us. They greeted every new band like that. We were the latest, great white English hopes, so we got the full groupie welcome. We thought, 'What is this all about?' We had been ambushed by female fans before, but we had never known them to be so blatant. They were walking up to us saying, 'Can I fuck you tonight?' We were going, 'Can we put our bags down first?'

We stayed at The Hyatt for about a week. We were playing gigs outside LA, but that was our base. One night, I was having a drink in the bar and in came Alice Cooper, Jeff Beck and Danny Hutton. Danny was one of the singers from Three Dog Night, who were a hugely successful vocal harmony band in the States. They all lived in LA so they knew the best haunts. I ended up going out with them. It was my introduction to LA nightlife. The four of us got totally plastered and went on a club crawl. We had a fantastic night, not that I remember much about it. I was out of my tree. I do remember one club we went to that refused us admission. It was a real trendy place on Sunset Strip. They said we were too pissed to get in. It turned out that Danny actually owned this venue. The bouncer on the door hadn't realised. Danny fired him on the spot.

We were fascinated by America and Americans, but we were also very wary of how we would be received by audiences over there. We had no idea how much they knew about us or how well our records had been selling. We had a very rude awakening. Our first show was opening for Humble Pie, which was Steve Marriott and Peter Frampton's band at the time. They were getting a big name in the States and they were great live. The gig was in San Diego, which is just outside LA. The place was vast. We had never seen an indoor venue like it. When it was empty, it was fuckin' huge. We couldn't imagine it full of people. We walked in and saw Humble Pie's equipment all set up. That was the first time we had ever seen a backline all miked up. No European venues did that. We couldn't believe the size of their equipment or of the PA system. Everything was on such a bigger scale than we were used to.

We watched Humble Pie's soundcheck. It was incredible. They had soundmen out front and every instrument on stage was properly miked-up. We had to get their crew to set our equipment up the same way. We had no choice. The place was so big that no one would have heard us otherwise. The venue was almost full by the time we went on stage and it was obvious that a lot of the crowd had turned up early to see us. Our reputation had preceded us. It was either that or people had seen the huge Slade billboards along Sunset Strip. One was just a picture of me in my top hat with huge beams of lights coming off it. I remember looking at it and thinking, 'My God, that's me. I'm a Hollywood billboard. I've made it on to Sunset Strip.'

We were all pretty nervous about the gig, but we got through it okay. There were no real problems as such. It was just a strange atmosphere. We went down okay, but it wasn't what we were used to. At home, we always tore the place apart. That night, we definitely didn't. Later, we realised why. The whole audience was stoned. They were all off their heads. It was the first time we had played in front of a stoned crowd and we weren't used to their laid-back ways. They were all sitting down, waiting to be impressed. Their attitude was, 'Hey, man, let's hear what you've got.' No matter what we had done, they weren't going to jump out of their seats and go crazy. We were too naive to suss the situation straight away. We knew people were smoking dope, because we could smell it in the arena. We didn't quite grasp how stoned they were though. The security had allowed them to smoke all the way through the gig. That was normal practice. In some places, the security were just as bad as the audience.

The other thing that was odd for us was the sound. We were used to being this big brash super-loud rock'n'roll band. Suddenly, we felt as though we were struggling to be heard. In this vast arena, our sound seemed tiny. That was something we had to get used to very quickly. When Humble Pie came on after us, we thought, 'We'll watch them and see what it's all about. We'll pick up a few tips.' Steve Marriott was a fantastic frontman anyway, but having already played a lot in the States, he knew how to handle American audiences. I stood at the side of the stage and studied what he did. He was amazing. After two songs, he had this whole crowd eating out of his hand. It was my first lesson in how to deal with a stoned audience.

The day after our opening date with Humble Pie in San Diego, we had to fly back to Britain. We were contracted to open a new venue in London. It was a big theatre in Mile End Road called The Sundown. We had been booked to do it for ages and it was just unfortunate that it coincided with the start of the tour. There was no way we could get out of it. Twenty-four hours after we'd arrived home, we had to get back on a plane for the States. It was the biggest distance we'd ever travelled between gigs. In the old days, we used to joke that our agents always booked our shows miles apart. They would give us one in Edinburgh, followed by one in Portsmouth. They never seemed to care how far apart they were. But compared to going to San Diego, then London, then back to LA, it had been nothing. We were clearly working on a whole new scale.

Humble Pie went down a storm that night. It was the same wherever they played. We were touring with them across the States, as well as doing some smaller, headline shows of our own. For us, it was great experience, but also quite disheartening. We soon realised what the likes of Humble Pie had that we didn't. They were doing lots of long guitar and drum solos, which were exactly what the stoned Yanks wanted to hear. They used to do sets that lasted for up to two hours, half of which were solos. We weren't that sort of act. We played four-minute rock-pop songs. We did small solos for effect. Dave would get up on a plinth and play for maybe three minutes on his own, but it was never the fifteen to twenty minutes American bands would do. Don also did a drum solo and Jim sometimes did a violin solo, but it was all rehearsed. It wasn't improvised jamming. We could have made it easy on ourselves and added longer solos to our set, but we were determined not to. It wasn't what we were into. That proved to be a big problem for us, because Americans do love their guitar heroes. That's why British bands like Led Zeppelin, Black Sabbath and Deep Purple became so big over there. We went down well in certain pockets of the country, but the laid-back sunshine cities like LA were much slower to accept us.

Another stumbling block for us in the States was the way we dressed. We could tell crowds were shocked by our colourful clothes as soon as we walked on stage. They didn't like them much. The Californians were like, 'Who are these guys? What the hell are they wearing?' We looked strange by anyone's standards, but compared to the likes of Humble Pie, who wore regulation jeans and t-shirts, we were doubly outrageous. The Yanks weren't used to bands dressing up at all. The only groups doing it were the black acts like Sly and The Family Stone, not the white rock acts.That was something else we weren't going to change though. We adapted our show to suit arenas, but that was the only concession we were prepared to make. We learnt how to use a bigger stage and to play to people on the tiers. After that, reactions to us improved, although we could never compete with Humble Pie. We toured with them for almost a month because Frank Barcelona was their agent too and he had set us up with them. It was a good introduction, but we were just dipping our toes into the water as far as the States was concerned.

It was only when we got to New York that we actually met Frank Barcelona for the first time. He was a huge man, physically very intimidating. He was also a typical flash American agent. One Sunday, he invited us up to his house in the hills on the outskirts of the city. It was a mansion. The thing about Frank was that his voice was like Marlon Brando in *The Godfather*, he sort of mumbled in a very deep voice. When we got to his house, we didn't know what to think. He was definitely a character. I'll never forget some of the things he said. I remember him talking to us about Vic Damone, who was a '50s crooner from Las Vegas. Frank loved him. He said, 'Heh, boys, I been in de music business a long time, but I never understand it. You get Vic Damone – great voice, boy looks good and the women love him. He not a superstar. I no understand it. You have Tony Bennett – bad toupee, walks like a trucker, can't sing as good. The man's a star!' That was Frank all over. He was the first high-powered American mogul we had met. For all the success we had had in Europe and all the people we had worked with, this was a whole new ball-game. America is so much bigger and there's so much more money involved. It certainly put our British success into perspective.

By the time we went to the States, we had broken just about every other country in the world. Obviously, we wanted to make it there, but it turned out to be a big struggle for us. It is the hardest territory for any British band to crack and we never really managed it. It was mainly because we wouldn't conform to what the Americans wanted. It was also because we were ahead of our time. We were doing a different act to other rock bands in America in the early '70s. In the early '80s, flamboyant outfits and raucous music became the thing. Bands like Kiss, that came to our shows, went on to form groups that were very much influenced by us and became huge stars in the '80s. That's when we had our biggest hits over there too. We hadn't been to the States for six years by then, but suddenly we came into fashion.

Throughout the mid '70s, the Yanks saw us as an album band rather than a singles act. We used to get a lot more play on FM radio than on AM. Back then, AM stations played singers like Carly Simon, James Taylor and Carole King. We didn't fit that format at all. Some territories made an exception. In New York and the Mid-West, they loved our brashness. We also did well in Detroit, Chicago and Cleveland – all the nitty-gritty cities. We had huge local hits in all those places, but we never had a hit across the whole country. In America, you could be massive on one coast and unheard of on another, because then there was no MTV.

The best example of a band who were huge in some places and nothing in others was ZZ Top. In their very early days, before they even had their beards, they were just a bar band in the southern States. We got to hear about them because their guitar player, Billy Gibbons, was Jimi Hendrix's favourite guitarist. Whenever Hendrix was in their neck of the woods, he used to go to whatever dive they were playing in just to see Billy Gibbons. For years, no one was bigger than ZZ Top in the southern States, but they didn't mean a thing anywhere else. We toured with them after they had had their first small hit outside the South. It was their first major tour of the northern States and they took us out as an opening act because we had a bigger following there than they did at the time. I think things changed for them straight after that tour. Their success didn't surprise me at all. They were a blues-based band, fantastic live. On stage, they usually wore jeans and cowboy hats. but if we were playing a big venue, they'd put on their rhinestone suits like real cowboys. This was in 1974 or 1975 and that was the sort of thing the Yanks wanted to see in those days.

During our first tour of the States, we began to pick up quite a bit of FM radio play with 'Mama Weer All Crazee Now', which had just been released. It was even a No.1 song in some areas, although nationally it only made the Top 50. Despite its success, we were always a rock act to the Yanks, never a pop act. We rather liked our rock status in America. At first, not having hits there didn't much bother us. Very few British bands were successful over there at the time anyway. Bolan had one hit with 'Get It On', but that was the only one he ever managed. He even had to change the title of it. In America, it was called 'Bang A Gong', because there was another song called 'Get It On' that had already been a hit.

For the first few weeks at least, we were too busy getting used to America and Americans to worry about how well our records were selling. As well as having to adapt our show to suit arenas, we were flying every day, which was a very weird experience. The whole country seemed weird. One of my lasting memories of that tour was going down to breakfast in the hotel on the first morning. I saw all these people eating huge steaks and piling up their plates with pancakes dripping with syrup and cream. I'd never seen anyone tuck into that type of food for breakfast. I just thought, 'It's a different world.' Which it was. It was like landing on another planet.

As well as supporting Humble Pie, we got to play a few smaller shows of our own. The first was at a little theatre just outside New York City. That was great. We could do our proper set and we went down a storm. It was the same in a lot of the heavy industrial areas like Milwaukee, Boston, Cleveland and Detroit. The crowds there reminded us of our audiences in the Midlands. New York was different, but for some reason, we built up a big fanbase there. We didn't like the city at all when we first went, because it was so frenzied. I think many people feel the same. We couldn't believe the way everyone was swearing and rushing around the whole time.

What we did love about New York was the food. It was the first time any of us had ever eaten proper pizza. We thought the food was the best thing about the city and we were determined to go out to eat as much as possible. One night, we said we wanted to go to an Indian restaurant. We had a guide to look after us and show us where to go. He thought we meant a Red Indian restaurant. He thought we wanted to eat buffalo. He'd never heard of our type of Indian restaurant, but he actually went out and found one. It was called Nirvana and it looked right over Central Park. We thought this was great – the four of us going for an Indian meal slap bang in the centre of New York City.

My best food discovery in New York was the cheesecake. Both Swin and I fell in love with it. Once, when we were on quite a long US tour, we bought a whole one in New York – it must have been eighteen inches wide – and took it on the road with us. You couldn't get anything like it in any other city. We tried to see how long we could go without eating it. It became a bit of a game really. We'd take it from the hotel fridge in the morning, on to the plane, then to the next city and another hotel fridge. It was semi-frozen all the time. We got through two-thirds of the tour before we could resist it no longer. We finally succumbed in a little town in the Mid-West. It was after a gig and we were bored. We got stoned and suddenly we had the munchies. That was the end of the line for the cheesecake. That was the sort of eccentric thing we were constantly doing to keep ourselves amused. We had a saying for it in the band. After a few months on the road, we'd say, 'The tour madness has set in.'

One of the good things about being in the States was that,

when we were in big cities like New York or LA, there were always great gigs to go to on our nights off. I saw Bob Marley and The Wailers' first ever American show at a little club called The Roxy on Sunset Strip. Hardly anyone over there had heard of Bob Marley back then. It was years before mainstream America discovered reggae. I was already a big Bob Marley and The Wailers fan. I had all their early albums, but I'd never seen them live. It was a brilliant gig, one of the best I've ever seen. I'll never forget it. The club was packed, mainly with Brits, and the atmosphere was electric. Marley was such a star. It was on nights like those that I really appreciated being in a band. It was a privilege to visit so many places and see so many things that most people never experience.

America was exciting, but it was also knackering, especially for me. I had to do six or seven interviews at radio stations every morning, then loads more with the press in the afternoon. It was never-ending. It didn't help that the Yanks could never understand our accents. They thought we were Australian. They'd say, 'What's the name of your band?' We'd go, 'Slade.' 'Slide?' 'No. Slade.' 'Slide?' And so it went on. They almost always thought we were Aussies. They loved our dialect, but they just couldn't get their heads around it. We ended up speaking so slowly all the time. After a few weeks, we even started using their sayings. Instead of 'Let's get pissed', it was 'D'ya wanna paaa-rty'. That became our catch phase on tour.

As a band, we were used to hard work, but America was particularly tough. It was non-stop business, twenty-four hours a day. Even the after-show parties were gauged to the hard sell. The record dealers, marketing men and radio jocks would all come down after gigs and expect us still to be working. We had to meet people even when we were knackered. We hadn't realised how much graft America was going to be. The problem was that, until we got there, we had no idea how vast the country actually was. We weren't so naive that we expected to arrive there and be loved straight away, but Chas had somewhat misled us.

That was always his way. He was never one to knock your confidence – never, ever. He always said, 'You're the greatest band in the world' or 'Noddy, you're the best singer I've ever heard.' He gave you immense confidence. He obviously knew it would be tough for us in the States, but he never told us that before we went.

We came back to Britain after that tour a much wiser band. Our shows were also a lot more impressive. We updated all our equipment, our PA system and our lighting. Every band who had toured the States did the same. I remember going to see Mott The Hoople play in Wolverhampton before we went over there. They had already spent time in America and when we came back, we understood where they had got their ideas from. Free and Status Quo were using the same tricks too. We all wanted to emulate US bands by making our sound bigger and better.

We were already a noisy band, but with our new PA system, we were shockingly loud. At the time, we came on stage every night to a song called 'Hear Me Calling'. It was a Ten Years After cover. We did a totally different version of it, which started off very quietly. That was an idea I had nicked from The Spencer Davis Group. It had such a great effect. I'd stand centre-stage, just gently playing the guitar for the first few minutes. That sucked people in. Jim and I then sang the first verse very low. You could see the crowd thinking, 'What the hell is this? Where's the volume gone?' Suddenly, we'd blast in this riff, with all three of us on guitar. All the sound and lights came on at once. The impact knocked people off their feet. British audiences weren't used to these huge PA systems that were all properly miked up. It was a new experience for them and it helped us to stand out. It made us seem even more over the top and extravagant.

We opened our show like that for years. We even recorded 'Hear Me Calling', but it didn't have the same impact on record. You had to hear it live. We later toured with Ten Years After in the States and their singer, Alvin

Lee, told us he had made more money out of us recording the song than he had with his own band. He was dead chuffed with us for that, even though Ten Years After were a huge act in America.

Our follow-up single to 'Mama Weer All Crazee Now' was 'Gudbuy T' Jane'. It was one of the easiest songs we ever recorded. We were in the studio finishing off some album tracks, when we found ourselves with half an hour to spare and nothing to do. Chas hated to waste studio time. He said, 'Haven't you got any other songs? Let's just lay down a basic track to whatever you've got and use up the time.' Jim and I didn't have anything really, except one song we had barely started, about a girl called Jane we had met in San Francisco. None of the others had heard it. We played what we had to Chas and he loved it. He said, 'Get this down on tape now. You've got 30 minutes.' While Jim was teaching the tune to Dave and Don, I went into the bog and finished the lyrics. I knew roughly what they were going to be because it was a true story.

Jane was a beautiful-looking girl who co-hosted a TV chat show we had been on in San Francisco. She could only have been sixteen. She didn't seem to do anything on screen. The interviews were all done by a bloke. Jane just sat next to him, stroking her long blonde hair. She never said one word on screen. On the day we were there, right before the show went on air, Jane lost what she called her "40s trip boots'. Really, they were just platform shoes. She thought they were original '40s shoes and she told us that she had paid a fortune for them. Apparently, the bloke she bought them from had told her they were genuine antique boots, but they were exactly the same as the ones in all the high-street shops back in Britain. She made this big fuss about how the show couldn't go ahead until she had found these bloody platforms. That's basically what the whole song was about. The lyric 'Got a kick from her '40s trip boots' referred to her kicking me up the arse. We were taking the piss out of her for losing her shoes and when she found them, she put them on and kicked me. She was a real loony, a typical

San Francisco hippy.

We recorded the song in two takes and virtually finished the entire track that afternoon. The next day, we put on some more guitars and a few backing vocals and Chas mixed it. He said, 'Lads, this is the next single.' It was Jim who came up with the title 'Gudbuy T' Jane'. I wanted to call it 'Hullo T' Jane'. That summed up the difference between me and Jim. He always went for the pessimistic point of view. I always went for the happy opposite. Put it this way, Jim's nickname with our road crew was the Midlands' Misery. On that occasion, I was out-voted. Everyone liked 'Gudbuy T' Jane', so that's what we called the song. Chas was still fine-tuning his plan for us to go in at No.1. We didn't do it with 'Gudbuy T' Jane', but as it turned out, we didn't have long to wait. The next year, we had three singles that all went straight into the charts at No.1.

In early 1973, we played our second UK concert tour. We took Suzi Quatro out with us as our opening act. She had just come to Britain and it was the first time she had ever performed here. She had barely got her first band together before the dates began. No one knew of her at all. Mickey Most had spotted her in Detroit, signed her up, brought her over and set her up with some English musicians. Mickey had been The Animals' record producer, so he was big mates with Chas. Mickey asked both us and Chas if, as a favour, we would take Suzi on tour with us to give her a feel of playing in front of an audience.

The second act on the bill was Thin Lizzy, who were then a three-piece. They had just had their first hit with 'Whisky In The Jar'. That was probably the most riotous tour we ever played. It was madness from start to finish. Suzi always kicked things off with a twenty-minute set. She still moans to me today about how little time we gave her. To be fair, she didn't have many songs. Plus, our audiences were notorious for giving the support acts a hard time. A lot of them were total hardcases. It didn't matter who the support act was – male or female, obscure or well-known. If our crowds liked them, they loved them. If they hated them, boy did they show it.

Suzi did really well under the circumstances. Looking back, I think it would have been fatal for her to have played longer. I've told her this several times since. Twenty minutes was perfect. No one knew any of her songs. She sort of admits now that we were right. Not long ago, she told me she had learnt so much from watching me on that tour. She said she learnt how to handle an audience and get them involved. Phil Lynott said exactly the same. All of Thin Lizzy used to stand at the side of the stage and watch us every night. I could tell when I saw them perform afterwards that they had been influenced by what we were doing.

Thin Lizzy were a great band even then. At the time, their set was very Irish rock. Suzi was doing mainly covers. She was also performing 'Can The Can'. That was her first single, which came out shortly afterwards. It went to No.1, so we obviously gave her career a big boost. We also found her a husband on that tour. We got her together with Lenny Tuckey, her guitar-player. I remember the very night it happened. She came and sat with me in the dressing room. She said, 'I think Lenny fancies me. What should I do? I don't know whether I should start seeing him or not.' They hadn't known each other very long. She obviously liked him, but she was too nervous to make the first move. I said, 'Suzi, just go for it.' A few days later, they got together at a party after a show in Plymouth. They were married not long after that. In the '90s, they split up and Suzi remarried. Lenny is now Dave and Don's manager.

I ended up becoming big pals with Phil Lynott on that tour. Phil was a madhead, into as much of everything that he could lay his hands on. In later years, he was renowned for his outrageous behaviour, but even then he was constantly stoned and a big drinker. He died ten years later from misuse of drugs, but by then he really had lived the rock'n'roll lifestyle. He had as many women, as much booze and as many drugs as anyone I ever knew.

Over the next few years, we toured with Thin Lizzy a lot, both in Britain and the States. In 1974, we had just begun an American tour with them when Phil was taken really ill. We were in Detroit. The doctor came to see him, then insisted he fly to New York for more tests. It turned out that Phil had hepatitis. It was the contagious type. We were all panicking. Everyone on the tour – including all the crew – had to go to the local hospital for a jab. It was one of the funniest sights ever. Dozens of us were taken into this room and told to stand in a long line. Then we all had to drop our trousers and bend over while the nurse went along jabbing everyone's arse. Let me tell you, it was not a pretty sight. We never forgave Phil for that.

It was after one night on that tour that I wrote the lyrics for 'Cum On Feel The Noize'. When we were on stage, the audience was chanting along so loudly to every song that I couldn't hear myself sing. The venue we were in was really echoey and the noise was bouncing off the walls. I originally called the song 'Come On Hear The Noize', but when I thought back on the gig, all I could remember was how I had felt the sound of the crowd pounding in my chest. 'Feel' was a much better word to describe it.

Even before the single came out, we knew it was going to be a monster hit. We had played it a few times on stage and it always sent the audience wild. In the days leading up to release, 'Cum On Feel The Noize' got pre-orders of 300,000. By the following week, it had another 200,000. It shot straight to No.1. Two weeks later, it was still there. It held Bolan's '20th Century Boy' at No.2, which Dave was particularly pleased about. I wasn't bothered about Bolan. We were the first band to go in at No.1 since The Beatles, that's what mattered to me. I remember the day we found out its position. From the pre-sales, we were pretty sure we had done it, but when we were told for certain, it was a fantastic feeling. Part of the success was down to Chas and his marketing plan, which had finally come to fruition. Mostly though, it was down to the strength of the song.

'Cum On Feel The Noize' has been covered by loads of bands. It's just a great rock'n'roll record.

We had a gig in Manchester on the day that we went to No.1. When we stepped on stage, the atmosphere was electric. The whole crowd knew about the chart position and they were just waiting for us to play the song. That same night, Manchester United had won some big Cup-game, so the whole city was celebrating. The place was fit to burst. It was one of the most memorable shows I've ever played. It was pandemonium. After that, our profile went crazy. We couldn't get anywhere near venues anymore. We had to be driven to and from every gig in cop vans.

One of the maddest nights was when we played Green's Playhouse in Glasgow. After the show, the cops picked us up and hid us in the back of their van. They told us we'd have to wait for a couple of hours, before they could get us into our hotel. They parked up on the banks of the River Clyde. We were starving, so we sent one of them out to get us fish and chips. We were all huddled in the back of the van, in total darkness and silence, freezing cold, munching on chips. It was hardly the glamourous lifestyle. In the end, the streets had to be cleared before we could get to the hotel. A lot of kids used to find out where we were staying, then camp outside all night. There could be hundreds of them still there in the morning. We had to devise tricks to get us in and out of places. All the fans recognised our Rolls-Royce limo, so we used to send the driver past the hotel doors on his own. The kids would chase the car, then we'd nip out of the police van and get inside.

We knew that being smuggled in and out of places was part and parcel of being a pop star, but we got sick of it pretty quickly. We liked the adulation, but we hated not being able to go to the shops or the cinema. I think even Dave found it tiresome after a while. The only places we could go out to and not get hassled were our local pubs back in the Midlands. People there had known us for years and most of them didn't treat us any differently.

After 'Cum On Feel The Noize' was such a big hit, we

began to attract a lot of real nutter fans. Fortunately, we very rarely got to meet them. By then, the tours were mayhem. It was far too chaotic to invite anyone backstage. That was the height of us being mobbed. It got dangerous on quite a few occasions. Thousands of fans were turning up at venues and hotels, waiting for us to either arrive or leave. They would throw themselves on top of the car, with no thought for their own safety. We often knocked people down trying to get away. They'd be banging on the windows. It's a frightening experience. When you're inside a car and there are thousands of mad kids outside, rushing at you all at once, it's pretty dodgy. It wasn't like it is today, where you drive into backstage car parks. In the States, where they were used to the rock'n'roll lifestyle, it was already like that, but in Britain, the stage door would back out on to a little alley and you could get trapped. Often we thought the car was caving in with people jumping on it. It was very hairy. Sometimes kids clung on to the roof or the bonnet for grim death and we couldn't shake them off. It became a military operation to get us in and out of venues and hotels. It was a nightmare.

All the mayhem made us realise how big a band we were. Apart from the reaction of the fans and knowing that we were getting No.1 records, we literally knew nothing of the outside world for a couple of years. We saw the inside of dressing rooms, hotels, tour buses, planes, TV and radio studios, recording studios and concert halls. I thought it was fantastic though. I was travelling the world first-class, getting all the women and booze I wanted and visiting cities I had hardly heard of. We had a hell of a time. We lost our privacy, that was the downside, but we made the most of what we had worked all those years for. We were determined to enjoy it while it lasted.

TOUR
MADNESS

8

In the middle of all the mayhem of hits and tours and trips to the States, I bought my first house. It was in Sutton Coldfield, on the outskirts of Birmingham, in a posh area next to the park I used to visit with my mates as a kid. It was exactly where I'd always said I'd move as soon as I had enough money. I specifically looked for a place on that estate. To be honest, I didn't really need a house. I was always away and if I wanted to go back to the Midlands, I could stay with my mum and dad. I didn't live in the place for years. I visited it for two weeks here and there, but I didn't properly move in. My parents looked after it. They used to go over once a week to clean and keep the garden up.

The house was actually built by the Birmingham City Architect. He had lived there himself, but he was selling it. I bought the place the moment it went on the market. It was a bungalow, which looked like a Scandinavian chalet. It had loads of windows and masses of light. The back wall was just one big pane of glass. It was like a glorified greenhouse, a real nightmare to clean. It was very odd looking, especially for those days. When I first saw it, I freaked. I thought, 'This is the sort of place a pop star should live.' The design was so off-the-wall. It was all triangular shapes and sloping ceilings. It wasn't a mansion, but it didn't look like any other house I had ever seen. Inside, it was all Canadian wood, even on the floors. I fell in love with it.

From day one, some of the neighbours hated me being there. When I bought it, the front garden was open to the

161

road. The first thing I had to do was get someone in to build a huge security fence with big gates. I was away so much that the place had to be secure and I didn't want kids to be able to see in. They still used to climb over the fence and nick stuff out of the garden, but it was quite an assault course for them.

At the time, I didn't have a steady girlfriend. Being constantly on the road, I had found that impossible. I was meeting loads of women and didn't have the time to commit to someone back home. Jim was married and both Dave and Don had girlfriends in Wolverhampton. Dave bought a house shortly after Jim and later got married to his girlfriend, who he's still with. Don bought a flat in Wolverhampton, but he split up with his girlfriend shortly after.

As we became more and more successful, our schedule got busier and busier. We were constantly recording and releasing records, as well as touring non-stop. We were going back to the States in short bursts every four or five months. Between those trips, we were playing Britain, Europe, Japan and Australia.

We did our first tour of Australia in early 1973. We went out there on a bill with lots of other bands and played at racecourses all over the country. The audiences were vast – at least 30-40,000 people at every show. We were the headliners. The other groups were Status Quo, Lindisfarne and Caravan – who were a real progressive rock group, nothing like any of the other acts on the bill – and a couple of Australian bands. We had no idea how popular we were over there. It wasn't until we arrived that we found out we had three singles in the charts at the same time. *Slade Alive* had been the No.1 album for six months. It had only dropped to No.2 when our next album, *Slayed*, came out and knocked it off the top. In those days, it was hard to keep up with how well your records were doing all over the world.

All the British acts went over to Australia on the same flight. It took us twenty-eight hours in total to get there and we were drinking all the way. By the time we landed, we were all totally pissed. As we got off the plane, we noticed loads of press and TV cameras gathered on the tarmac. They filmed us coming down the steps. As a promotional gimmick, they had brought along a huge wheelbarrow filled to the brim with Fosters lager. They knew we were a big drinking band and they wanted us to finish this whole barrowful of beer. We had a go, but there was no way we could drink it. That was our first step on Australian soil.

Every date on that tour was like playing a festival. In fact, it was like playing a British festival. While we were there, the country experienced the worst rain it had had for twenty years. Everywhere was flooded. Only the Melbourne gig got good weather. On that day, Status Quo came on as usual as the second to last band, right before us. During their set, the sun was really strong. It was shining straight on to the stage. They had forgotten to put on sunscreen and by the time they'd finished, they were all really burnt. It was hysterical. Their faces were bright red for the rest of the tour, even though everywhere we went it was pouring with rain. We really took the piss out of them for that.

Quo were a brilliant band to go on the road with, great fun. They were already good friends of ours and both them and Lindisfarne were big drinkers, so we had a riot together. Just before we went to Australia, I had spent a day in London recording hundreds of trailers for all the local radio stations out there to promote the gigs. Every morning, all the bands poured out of the hotel and on to the bus for the airport with massive hangovers – there wasn't one night on that tour that we didn't have a huge after-show party. Everyone would be sitting there bleary-eyed, nursing their heads and the driver would turn on the radio. The first thing everyone heard was my chirpy voice doing these trailers, then a run of our records. With three singles and two albums in the charts, we were on almost non-stop. Quo would be going, 'Oh, no. Not bloody Noddy again.' I'd be on air screaming, 'Hiya possums! It's Noddy Holder and you can catch us tonight in Sydney,' or wherever it was. We had a raucous old time. We were banned from one airline for having a food fight. We were all throwing rolls and bits of chicken at each other. Tour madness had set in. It caused us a lot of problems because we ended up having to drive to a couple of cities, which we really didn't need.

Chas was the only one who didn't mind us being banned from whatever airline it was. He absolutely hated flying and the Aussie pilots really were awful. They were like kamikazes. They just dropped on to the runway with a big bang and threw all the passengers around. Once, after a particularly bad landing, Chas jumped out of his seat and charged up into the cockpit. He grabbed the pilot. He was screaming at him, ready to beat him up. He was going, 'You fuckin' silly bastard. You nearly killed me.' The whole plane could hear him. We were just sat there, laughing.

We were usually pretty sensible about drinking, in that we stayed sober until after the gigs. We might have one beer to calm our nerves beforehand, but we very rarely got pissed before we played. By then, the whole band was drinking. When we first became successful, Don had started having the odd glass of champagne or whatever. He ended up worse than the rest of us. We did throw fantastic parties though. We blew a lot of our money touring, but we didn't mind. It was there to be enjoyed and we were making more than enough, more than we'd ever dreamed of.

Another big expense for us was our equipment. We used to ship it around the world with us. Most bands went to a country and hired gear locally. We wanted to be seen in the best possible light in every country. We had a big PA system and lighting rig and we were determined to use it at every gig. We knew we couldn't hire equipment of the same standard, so we took it with us. We even shipped it to Australia, which cost us an absolute fortune. At first, we took it to America too. Eventually, we had a replica system built over there. Other bands told us we were mad to spend so much money, but if it made us look and sound better, we thought it was worth it.

Straight after the Australian jaunt, we went to Japan for the first time. Naturally, our equipment came with us. A lot of it was brand new. We had just been given some gear by a British firm. It was a new design and we were testing it out for them. At venues in Japan, there are union rules which say that only local crews can set up your equipment. At the first gig, our roadies showed them how to do it, but they actually put it together. After just one night, the Japanese crew learned it all, down to the minutest detail. They dismantled the entire set afterwards and had it back in the truck in forty minutes. They were so efficient, it was amazing. At the second gig, we turned up to see them closely inspecting the equipment. They had the backs off all the amplifiers and were taking lots of photos. They were obviously impressed. We were boasting, saying, 'You've got nothing like this over here, have you?' One of them said, 'No. But we soon will have.'

Japanese audiences were weird for us. The security at the venues was very tight and there were laws to prevent people from standing up in the seats. That was no good for our show. We would actively encourage everyone to get up on their feet from the start. We caused riots nearly every night. Kids loved us for letting them break the rules. The first chance they got, they were up. We got into a lot of trouble with promoters and we were constantly shelling out for damages. A lot of the venues had never experienced such bad behaviour.

None of us had ever been to Japan before, but we loved it. Everyone was so eager to please. They went out of their way to make sure we had a good time. After one show, the promoter took me to a geisha house. Dave refused to come because he said he hated the food there. Whenever we were taken out to a gorgeous restaurant for a meal, Dave would make his excuses and head off to Burger King or McDonalds on his own. He really missed out on the geisha house. It was amazing. There were all these beautiful women who would take you off into rooms that looked like tropical gardens. There were waterfalls and streams running through them. It was another world.

The Japs hated Westerners to see anything sleazy about their culture. That whole side of the country was kept very much under cover. We had a driver over there who took us to all the gigs. One night in Tokyo, when we were heading back to the hotel, we told him we were fed up of the tourist sights in the city and asked him to take us to the sort of place where only locals hung out. We said, 'We're always going to posh restaurants and flash discos, but we want to see the other side of Japan. We want to experience the real nitty-gritty.' He was shaking his head. He said, 'Oh no, I couldn't possibly take you to where the locals go. My boss will fire me.' I said, 'We won't tell, if you don't.' Then we threatened to strip all his clothes off and throw them out of the car window. He had no choice, so he took us to this club. It was obvious as soon as we walked through the door that they had never had Westerners in there before. Everyone was sitting around drinking. It was like a gambling den, very sleazy, full of criminals. The place went silent when we entered. Not only were we Westerners, but we had long hair and we were wearing our colourful clothes. We were quite pissed as well, because we'd all been out for dinner and drunk loads of sake.

We ordered a round of drinks and sat down. A few minutes later, the staff from behind the bar all appeared in front of us. They were transvestites and had gone off and changed into women's clothes. They put on a cabaret show just for us, right next to our table. It was fantastic. They were doing Shirley Bassey songs, but in Japanese. They thought it was wonderful that Westerners had come to their club. They were just miming to the tapes, but they were really going for it. We couldn't understand a word but we had a great night. We must have been there until seven o'clock in the morning.

I fell in love with Japanese girls when we were over there. I think all of us did. They were great fun. I went out with one in particular. She was sent to me as a present from the bass player in The Faces, a Japanese guy called Tetsu, who had taken over from Ronnie Lane. She came to my hotel room on the day we arrived in Japan. She knocked on my door. When I opened it, she said, 'Tetsu sends you present.' I said, 'Yeah? What is it?' She said, 'Me.' That was all she could say. 'Me, present.' She couldn't speak any other words of English. She was beautiful though. I took her with me on the whole tour. We had a brilliant time, despite the language barrier. Let's just say we worked out a way to communicate. We pointed to things. She was smashing.

We had a few hits in Japan, but we were never really huge there. They loved our flamboyance, but musically, we weren't their bag. They like either out-and-out heavy metal or total pop. We were neither. They couldn't quite get to grips with that. The oddest success we had there was when 'Cum On Feel The Noize' was covered by the Japanese equivalent of Cliff Richard. I think his version went to No.1. To be honest, it didn't bear much resemblance to the original. Had we not been told what it was, I don't think we would have guessed. It certainly wasn't a heavy rock song by the time this bloke had finished with it.

Straight after Japan, we went back to the States. One of our first dates over there was in New York. We played a great gig. The next day, there was a review of the show in the *New York Times*. It was one of the funniest things I ever read about us. It said, 'Slade took to the stage, four horrible Englishmen with a singer whose voice sounds like a fingernail going down a blackboard. To think Britain sent us The Beatles and now they send us THIS!' We got that sort of reaction all the time from the serious papers over there. They didn't like us one little bit, but reviews like that didn't bother us at all. Far worse had been written about us in Britain when we were skinheads. Plus, we were used to critics either loving us or loathing us. Such reactions were almost always based on how we looked, not how we played. It was different with the music press. They under-stood what we were trying to do and were usually very positive. We knew it would be the same all the way through our career. On the inside of the *Slade Alive* album sleeve, we had printed loads of our reviews, both good and bad, because that summed us up perfectly. Very few people thought we were just okay. They were either mad fans or they couldn't stand us.

Years later, we found out that Kiss had been in the audience at that New York show. This was before they had even formed a band. Apparently, we blew them away. They loved what we were doing on stage and decided to use it themselves, but make it even more over the top. To their credit, they admitted themselves that they had based their show on ours. Of course, by the time Kiss came along, that was what the Americans wanted. We just gave it to them too early.

During that tour, we played at our first American festival. It was in Fresno. It was one of the only places on the west coast where we built up quite a big following. The festival was to be headlined by Sly and The Family Stone, which was a pretty weird act for us to play with. I was a huge fan and I was looking forward to seeing them, although by then they did have a pretty bad reputation. They were notorious for turning up to gigs either really late or not at all and always out of their heads.

We went on right before them and by the end of our set, they hadn't turned up. We could see the promoter standing at the side of the stage, waving to us. He was going, 'Keep playing, boys. Sly and The Family Stone aren't here yet. Carry on, carry on.' We'd already done an hour, so we had to resort to lots of very old songs which we hadn't performed for years. We just kept playing and playing. We were on for over two hours. The crowd must have wondered if we were ever going to finish. Eventually, Sly and The Family Stone arrived. Their show was one of the biggest disappointments of my life. I had never seen them live and they were truly awful. This was the latter part of their career and they were so stoned that their music was a shambles. They still looked fantastic though. They all had huge Afros and totally over-the-top clothes. You could tell that if they had been even a little compos mentis, they could have been great. We met them afterwards for a drink in the bar, but they were too out of it to talk any sense at all. They really did seem to be on another planet.

We went back to Fresno several times after that and we got to know loads of people who lived there. There were two girls in particular who we always met up with. They weren't exactly groupies, just big fans of the band. They had first come to see us in San Francisco, then flown down to our next show in Fresno. After that gig, we were all going back to the airport, so we offered them a lift in our limo. I remember Peter Kauf, our American manager, saying to them, 'I don't understand you American girls. All you ever do is listen to music, get high and fuck.' One of them said, 'Yeah! And that's the way we like it.' Those girls came out with some great lines. They were always good fun to have around. Fans like that made us feel welcome when we went back to the same cities. We'd go out to eat with them and they'd take us to local clubs and parties. Just seeing a few familiar faces stopped us getting homesick.

When we used to tour the States on a regular basis, I got into collecting American police badges. Don't ask me why. I was just fascinated with cop badges. I think it came from watching movies as a kid. American cops always looked the bee's knees. They were like cowboys with their gleaming badges. I loved the way they used to swagger around at our shows. At every venue, I'd try to talk one of them into giving me a badge either off their tunic or their hat. They'd say 'Oh no, man. Can't give you that.' I'd go, 'Give me it and you can have a bottle of Scotch from the dressing room.' That usually did the trick. They would pretend they'd had a badge ripped off by the crowd and, in exchange, I'd give them a free bottle of whisky.

There was one cop I got to know quite well over the years. I'd see him on almost all of our tours. The first time I met him was when we played a club in Asbury Park, which is Bruce Springsteen's home town in New Jersey. I got chatting to him in the dressing room and he gave me his badge. We gave him the nickname Officer Dibble, like the copper off *Top Cat*. He loved it. He looked just like him and talked like him too. I could never remember his real name. When he walked into the dressing room, we'd all say, 'Oh, Officer Dibble. How's it going?'

After I got friendly with him, I asked him for a state cop's badge. They're impossible to get hold of. Officers can't afford to give them away, because the authorities are very strict about issuing them with new ones. Dibble wouldn't give me his on that occasion, but the next time we met, he pulled a spare one out of his pocket. 'That's for you,' he said. 'It's a present.' I couldn't believe he'd got me one. It turned out he had written to the President of the United States – which at that time would have been Nixon – and requested one for me. Nixon had sent me a state cop's badge. I was stunned. Hats off to Officer Dibble. What a guy!

I started getting bullets off the cops too. They gave me them out their belts. I don't know why I wanted them. They were just mementos. Why do people collect anything? It was a hobby. I guess it was a challenge for me to see how much stuff I could blag.

The police always used to come backstage at our shows, looking for dope. They very rarely found any. We weren't that stupid. When they realised we had nothing, they'd go out into the crowd and bust the kids for their dope. Then they'd bring it backstage for a smoke. That was a favourite trick of theirs. On one tour, just before a big show in Philadelphia, loads of cops were milling around backstage. I was in the dressing room with Swin, our tour manager, and a Scot called Robbie Wilson, who was one of our road crew. The pair of them disappeared for a couple of minutes and I decided to play a trick on them. I asked one of the cops to handcuff me to the door. I said, 'When they come back in, tell them you've busted me for dope.' When Swin and Robbie saw me, their faces dropped. Swin said, 'Oh my God! What are you arresting him for?' One of the cops says,

'Sorry, man. We found some dope on him. We gotta take him in. He'll be spending the night behind bars.' Robbie and Swin were shitting themselves. Chas wasn't at the show and there was no way they could go back and tell him it hadn't taken place because I'd been nicked. The rest of the band were there, all in on the joke, trying not to laugh. Swin and Robbie took the two cops outside for a word. We could hear them offering bribes to let me go.

It was a mad gig that night, one I definitely wouldn't have wanted to miss. We were closing the show on a bill which included The Eagles, Stevie Wonder and Lou Reed. Lou Reed's set was fantastic, but for all the wrong reasons. He was so out of his tree that he had to be carried on stage, dumped on a stool and given a guitar. He played two songs, then he had to be carried off, because he kept toppling over. He was terrible. He couldn't remember any of the words to his songs. This was at Philadelphia Spectrum, which held 20,000 people, so it was a really important gig. He was just so stoned – totally gone. When they carried him off, he was still on his stool, attempting to sing. It was brilliant. He was that bombed, that he hadn't noticed he wasn't in front of an audience anymore.

Someone we had quite often as our opening act in the States was Iggy Pop. Iggy was a lunatic, totally mad. This was in his real drug-addled days. We couldn't believe some of the things he did on stage. Every night, he'd jump into the audience and ask people to cut him with knives. Sometimes, he'd get them to hit him with chairs. By the end of his set, he'd be black and blue. Then he'd come back to the hotel, go up to his room and overdose on some sort of dope. It was almost a nightly occurrence. We'd still be in the bar when the ambulance arrived. We'd say, 'Oh, they're here to get Iggy again.' It was no big deal.

Despite all his problems, we loved touring with Iggy, because he was perfect for our audience. We often found ourselves playing with bands who didn't suit our fans at all. That said, we did a gig with Santana one night and it was brilliant. We were dreading it beforehand. We thought it would be a disaster. Slade and Santana seemed such a mismatch, if ever there was one. We were wrong. We went down a storm with their fans and they did with ours.

Another strange gig we played was with King Crimson and The Strawbs. You couldn't get three more different bands on the same bill. The Strawbs played first and went down okay, but not great. They were virtually unknown in the States though, so they didn't expect too much. Next up was King Crimson. Their frontman was Robert Frith, who I now know really well because he's married to Toyah. He's a smashing bloke, but a real eccentric. He's like an old English gent. King Crimson's music was quite complicated and clever and when they played, Robert would sit on a stool with his guitar. That audience that night was more or less a fifty/fifty split of their fans and ours. While King Crimson were on, our fans were shouting, 'Boogie, boogie.' That was the phrase they always used when they wanted to party. You could tell that it was pissing Robert off. After a couple of songs, he could stand it no longer. He got up off his stool, walked to the microphone and, in his really posh voice, said, 'We have no intention of boogie-ing.' It was one of the best lines I've ever heard in my life – the perfect put-down. I was standing at the side of the stage and I fell about laughing. It just summed Robert up.'

There were always mad things happening to us in the States. It just seemed to go with the territory. We even managed to get ourselves into strange scrapes in Canada, which is generally quite a well-ordered country. Once when we were on tour there, I ended up saving two girls' lives. It was on one of our nights off. Swin and I had gone to a bar, which had a back room where you could play pool. We were halfway through a game against a couple of locals, when suddenly all the fire alarms went off. Swin and I were going, 'Doesn't that mean there's a fire? Shouldn't we get out of here?' The locals said, 'Don't pay any attention. They're always going off. It's just the cigarette smoke.' Five minutes later, there was smoke billowing into the room. The place was going up in flames and we were stuck in this back room. The only way out was straight though the fire. Everyone was putting their coats over their heads and making a run for it. As I was charging through the flames, I heard screaming coming from the women's toilets. I thought, 'Bloody hell, someone's stuck in there.' I couldn't just ignore it. I ran back and kicked down the door. There were two girls in there and they couldn't get out. They were terrified. I turned on all the taps, soaked the three of us with water, then dragged them outside. The next day, it was in all the Canadian papers about how I'd saved these two girls' lives. Then the British press got hold of the story and it was in loads of papers back home. Both birds gave me a shag afterwards, as a way to say thanks. It was definitely worthwhile going to their rescue.

I saved another girl's life in New York, although that wasn't by choice. She was a real big Slade fan and she used to come to loads of our gigs, all over the east coast. One night, we played in Philadelphia, then drove back to New York, because that's where we were based. When we got to our hotel, it was very late, so I went straight up to my room. I walked in and saw this particular girl sitting on the end of my bed. I recognised her because I'd chatted to her quite a few times at shows. She'd always seemed perfectly nice. We weren't friends or anything though. I was furious when I saw her in my room. I said, 'What the hell are you doing here? How did you get in?' It turned out she'd sneaked in unnoticed when the maid was cleaning the room. She said, 'Can I stay for a bit?'. I said, 'No, you can't. I'm tired and I'm going to bed. You've got to go.' She asked if she could use the toilet before she left. I said, 'Fine. Go ahead.' She went in and locked the door. Ten minutes later, she was still in there. I started banging on the door, telling her to come out. There was no reply, no sound at all. I didn't know what to do. I called Swin for some help. He came round and the pair of us stood there threatening her through the door. There was still no sound. In the end, we had to break the door down. She was lying over the toilet seat and she'd slit her wrists. There was blood everywhere. We called the hotel manager and he called the paramedics. Everyone was trying to hush the thing up. We didn't want any bad publicity and neither did the hotel. The paramedics came to my room, bandaged her wrists and carted her off. We never saw her again after that.

If it wasn't mad fans getting us into trouble, it was usually our crew. Keeping them in check wasn't easy. We had characters like JJ, Charlie, Haden and Robbie Wilson who in particular, was a nutcase. He was a real hardcore Glaswegian, a real character and a very big drinker. He was forever getting thrown in jail when we were in the States. Once, he got done for speeding and he gave the cops so much cheek when they pulled him over, that they sent him straight to jail. This was in LA. When his case got to court, the judge let him come back out on the tour, but whenever we had any time off, he had to go back to LA to serve a bit more of his sentence.

In New Orleans, we saw our first shooting. There was actually a gun fight in the street in broad daylight. As soon as it started, everyone around us dropped to the ground. We were so green we just stood there and watched. Peter Kauf was with us. He was flat on the pavement, screaming, 'What the hell are you doing? Get down. Now!' We were so stunned we couldn't move. It was unbelievable, just like the movies.

Once, we went out to the States straight after a long tour of Europe. We did eighteen shows on the trot, without a day off. When we were in either Dallas or Houston – I don't remember which – my voice pegged out. It was the first time I had ever had a problem with it. I couldn't talk, let alone sing. It was simply a case of overwork. The record company thought it would help if I went to see a voice coach. I don't sing the proper way. I sing from my throat, like most rock musicians. They recommended a specialist in New York. By the time I got there, my voice was a lot better, but the record company insisted I go anyway, just to make sure there was no serious damage. I knew it was a waste of time as soon as I showed up at this bloke's surgery.

When I was sitting in the waiting room, I could hear one of his other clients singing. She was an actress from *West Side Story*, a big Broadway star. She was doing all the scales and she was note-perfect. When she left, I went in. The coach was like a mad professor. He was really old with grey hair. He said, 'So you have a problem with your throat, Mr Holder. I have to hear how you sing before I can tell you what's wrong. Please give me an example.' I said, 'Okay. Play me an A-chord on the piano.' He played and I sang the opening bars to 'Get Down and Get With It'. It's a real raunchy rock intro and I blasted it out. I could see him start to shake as soon as the words came out of my mouth. When I'd finished, he just sat there for a while. Then he turned to me and said, 'How long have you been singing like that Mr Holder?' I said, 'Oh, about thirteen years.' He said, 'If you've been singing like that for thirteen years, Mr Holder, I'm afraid there's nothing I can do for you. Please go and don't come back.'

In June of 1973, we played our biggest ever concert tour of Britain. As usual, it was mayhem. We had just released a new single, 'Skweeze Me, Pleeze Me'. It was the follow up to 'Cum On Feel The Noize' and it became our second single to go straight in at No.1. On those dates, we had the Sensational Alex Harvey Band opening for us. We had known them for a long time, from our days of playing Scotland with the 'N Betweens. They were a brilliant live band, but Alex, their singer, could be a terror. He was getting on a bit, even in those days. He'd been in rock bands for years and years and he knew the score about being a support act. Crowds always gave you some flak. Our audiences were particularly bad for that. If they didn't like a band, they made it quite clear from the start. Whenever Alex got any hecklers, he'd just insult them. He'd wind whole crowds up on purpose, if he felt like it. I think he enjoyed alienating people. He and his band put on a very unusual show. It was incredibly visual. Once you saw it, you never forgot it. They got mixed reactions on our tour, but three months later, they had their first hit record, so it did them a lot of good exposure-wise.

There were two places that Alex was really dreading playing with us. The first was in our home-town of Wolverhampton. He needn't have worried. He went down a storm there, much better than he did in Glasgow, which was his home-town. That was a terrible show for his band. I've no idea why. The crowd just didn't take to them. It was very odd. The other gig Alex was not looking forward to at all was the last nights of the tour in London. We had sold out Earl's Court. Earl's Court was an exhibition centre and we were scheduled to be the first rock band ever to play there. We were certainly the first group ever to book it. In the end, David Bowie beat us to playing there. He booked it after us, but his show took place a few days ahead of ours. There had never been an indoor concert playing to so many people in Britain before.

On the night, Alex and I hid behind the backstage scenery and watched the whole crowd file in. It was mad. There were 18,000 people and they were all dressed like Slade. There were loads of top hats with mirrors and silver-clad Dave look-a-likes. You could imagine what it must have been like all over London, with them getting on tubes and buses heading for Earl's Court. I remember thinking that if Martians had landed there that night, they'd have got straight back into their spaceships and never returned. I just stood there watching it all with Alex. I'll never forget what he said. He turned to me and went, 'If that lot boo tonight, it'll be the loudest boo there's ever been.' That was the thing about Alex. He had a great sense of humour, whatever the circumstances.

When we played Earl's Court, 'Skweeze Me, Pleeze Me' was still at No.1. It was a great gig, like the icing on the cake for us. We had never been more popular. We felt like we were on top of the world. Two days later, we came back down to earth with a bang. I had gone back to the Midlands to visit my mum and dad and I was staying over at their house. At 4 o'clock in the morning, the phone rang. It was

Don's dad. His voice was shaking and I could tell he was trying to stop himself sobbing. He told me that Don had been involved in a horrific car crash and that the doctors had given him twenty-four hours to live. Obviously, I didn't sleep a wink all night. First thing in the morning, I went to the hospital with Don's brother, Derek.

It turned out that both Don and his girlfriend, Angela, had had an accident in Don's big white Bentley. He had gone to pick Angela up at the club in Wolverhampton where she worked. That was at about 2 o'clock in the morning. They were heading home, out of town. No one knew for sure what had happened, but the car had swerved off the road and ploughed down a huge wall by the side of a school. Both of them had been thrown right through the windscreen. Angela died instantly. I went to see the Bentley a few days later and it looked like a concertina. It was built like a bloody tank, but it had been crushed right up on itself.

When we got to the hospital, Don was in the intensive care unit. He had pipes and tubes attached to every part of his body. His head had been shaved and there was a huge crack across the top where it had been cut open. He was covered in deep cuts and black bruises. He was sort of semi-conscious, just barely awake, but not aware of anything. To see the state of him, you wondered how he was still alive. His brother and I walked out of the room and I just burst into tears. We couldn't speak. It was awful. We were sure he was about to die.

Six weeks later, Don was back on his feet. It was incredible. He made a miraculous recovery. Twenty-four hours after the accident, instead of getting worse, he began to get better. Every day, there was a marked improvement in his condition. Physically, he was a really strong bloke. He wasn't big-built, but being a drummer, he was very fit and powerful. He had lost his short-term memory – which is common after accidents like his – as well as his sense of taste and smell. Even today, he can't smell or taste a thing. His memory is still a bit dodgy too, but nowhere near as bad as it was then. His long-term memory was never affected. He could chat to you in minute detail about stuff that had happened to him as a kid, but recent years were wiped right out.

Only a few days after Don's accident, Dave went on holiday. To be precise, he went on honeymoon. We were scheduled to have a week off after the Earl's Court shows. No one knew this at the time, but Don and Angela and Dave and his girlfriend, who was called Jan, had all planned to go to Mexico together. They were going to have a double wedding out there.

When everyone was back in the country, we had to decide what to do about the band. At first, we didn't know if Don would ever play again. If he hadn't been able to, I was ready to end it there and then. There was no way I would have replaced him. Slade wouldn't have been the same without Don. I don't know how the others felt about that, because we never really discussed it. As far as I was concerned, there wasn't any need. No Don meant no Slade – end of story.

By the autumn, we were due to be back in the States. First though, we were booked to play two gigs on the Isle Of Man. I wasn't sure about doing them, but Chas insisted they go ahead. He said, 'They'll be good for you. They'll help you get over what's happened and show the public that you're not giving up as a band.' So we did them. Clearly, Don couldn't play, so we got Jim's younger brother to stand in for him. He was a drummer in another band and he already knew all the songs. I think our audience appreciated the fact that we'd made an effort to fulfil our commitments, but it still felt strange.

Six weeks after the accident, on his doctor's advice, we got Don back in the studio. We were told that would be the best thing for him. We had some songs written for the next album and we decided to try to get them finished before we left for the States. We wanted to see how Don would cope with recording. We had been warned that it would be months before he could play properly again, but he proved everyone wrong. He must have used real force of mind, because he healed himself so quickly. He was desperate to play again, even though he could only walk with sticks and his head was still shaved. The main problem was his memory. He couldn't remember any tunes. When we were putting down new songs, as I was singing my part, I'd have to tell Don though his headphones what he was supposed to be playing. I'd be going, 'Don, get ready for the drum roll. . . Okay, now it's the tom-toms.' He could do it then. However, after he played it once, he forgot it all over again. It was the same with all the old hits. Once he got the intro, he was off and running. He just needed a prompt at the start.

For a couple of years, working with Don was a nightmare. He gradually got better and better, but it was very long hard road. It wasn't just in the studio that his memory loss was frustrating, it was all the time. On tour, he'd phone me up at night to ask what time we were leaving for the airport or wherever the next morning. I'd tell him 9 o'clock. Ten minutes later, he'd phone up and ask the same question. I'd tell him again. Ten minutes later, the same. I'd be screaming, 'Don, I just fuckin' told you. It's 9 o'clock.' I really had to lay into him. I was always the person the whole band relied on to know what we were doing. They all called either me or the tour manager to find out what the arrangements were. I had to be very hard on Don to drill it into him what he kept forgetting. He had no idea he'd called me three or four times. He'd apologise for forgetting, put the phone down, then half an hour later, he'd call again.

In the end, we had to get Don to write everything down. Before he went to bed, he'd get out his diary and write, 'Don, you're in Manchester. Today, you have to meet the band in the lobby at 8am. You have pack your stuff because we're leaving for London . . .' When he woke up in the morning, the first thing he'd do was look in his diary to find out where he was. That's how he lived for years. He wasn't too bad when he was at home, but if he was in another city, he was a dead loss.

I hated having to be tough with Don. His memory loss

was hellish for us, but we couldn't begin to imagine what it must have been like for him. Suddenly, his independence had been taken away from him. He had to rely on other people twenty-four hours a day. Before the accident, Don was the most punctual person I've ever met. He'd turn up early for everything. Now, he was getting to places an hour too soon. On top of everything, he'd not only lost his girlfriend, he had no memories of her at all. He didn't even know who she was in photos until you told him. Her parents blamed Don for the accident, but he wasn't the one driving. At least, that was what the court concluded at her inquest. No one knew for sure who was driving, because both of them were flung so far from the car. But, apparently, a taxi driver outside the club had seen a woman get behind the wheel and a man get into the passenger seat. Don couldn't remember a single detail about that night. He tried everything to bring his memory back. He tried hypnosis. He even had a specialist fly over from California to treat him. None of it did any good. Later, he began to have brief flashbacks. He always said he thought he could see a car pulling out of a side-road, making them swerve into the wall and then speeding off. There was never any proof to back that up though.

Considering what Don had been through, it was a miracle he survived at all, nevermind played the drums again. He eventually came through it okay, but it was a big shake-up for the band. It was front-page news in all the papers on the day that it happened. Everyone thought that Slade was over. There was a good chance we would have called it a day. If Don hadn't got back up to scratch so quickly with his playing, we would have finished.

The few weeks we had in the studio in London really strengthened Don up. We thought, 'If he can play as well as this already, we should try taking him to the States to see how he copes with a tour.' We went over for four weeks. Don coped brilliantly. By the end of it, his playing was more or less back to its best, although we still had to coax him through all the shows. While I was announcing a song, Jim would have to walk over to Don and tell him how the tune started.

When we came back from America, we went straight out on a European tour. Don was almost back to full strength by then. He'd even makes jokes about his memory. Years later, he'd use it to his advantage. If he had arranged to meet a girl and he changed his mind, he'd say, 'I'm sorry I didn't turn up. I've got a bad memory.' You never knew whether he'd genuinely forgotten or not.

Don's accident gave us all a good kick up the backside. We realised how quickly everything we'd worked for could be taken away from us. We had reached this pinnacle of success with the Earl's Court shows and our singles were going into the charts at No.1. It was phenomenal. Suddenly, we nearly lost it all in one day. That certainly made me appreciate what we had. It also put our status into perspective. If we had ever become big-headed about Slade, we couldn't be after that. None of it meant a toss. We were just a working rock band, fortunate to have had a lot of success. It wasn't until after the European tour that we decided for definite to carry on. After six months or so, things were almost back to normal, although they'd never be quite the same again.

I'M

READY FOR MY

CLOSE-UP

9

In September 1973, while we were away in the States, Polydor put out 'My Friend Stan' as our next single. It was one of the songs we had recorded in the studio in London just after Don's accident. It was never intended to be a single, just an album track, but Chas wanted us to release a new record as soon as possible. Polydor had already told us that they definitely wanted a Slade single out at Christmas time. 'My Friend Stan' was to be a stop-gap until then. It brought our strange spelling of song titles to an end. We never bothered with it after that. It also broke our run of No.1s, although it did do far better than we had expected. It peaked at No.2.

We had never done a Christmas single before. We'd had songs in the charts around that time – both 'Coz I Luv You' and 'Gudbuy T'Jane' had come out in November and sold well over Christmas, but they weren't specifically aimed at that market. When Polydor said they wanted to release a single in mid-December, we decided to make it an actual Christmas record. Until then, hardly any bands had written songs about Christmas. A few artists did in the '50s, but by the '70s, it was novelty records which were associated with that time of year. Rolf Harris' 'Two Little Boys', Benny Hill's 'Ernie' and Little Jimmy Osmond's 'Long-Haired Lover From Liverpool' had all been recent Christmas No.1s.

As soon as Jim and I sat down to work on an idea for the single, Jim suggested that we resurrect a song I had written way back in 1967. I have no idea what made him suddenly think of it. He just remembered that the chorus had sounded a bit festive. It was actually the first tune I had ever tried writing on my own. I came up with it when we were going through our hippyish phase. I did think it was a good song at the time, but we weren't recording our own material back then, so I had never done anything with it. We ended up using the chorus and the middle-eight of the song. The chorus was quite psychedelic. The original lyric was, 'So won't you buy me a rocking chair to watch the world go by, buy me a looking glass to look me in the eye-eye-eye'. The verse part wasn't commercial enough – at least, not the way we remembered it – so Jim came up with an alternative. He took a verse from another song he was writing and slotted it in. We'd often chop and change parts and jumble them around until finally they fitted together. Jim was a good musician, he could come up with melody lines and he'd hear a good song and retain it for months. Quite often we'd pinch bits of other people's songs without even realising it, so we'd end up re-working songs over and over until we got it right.

By the time we'd finished messing around with my old '60s song, we knew we were on to a winner. It was exactly what we had been looking for – a very commercial tune with a big hook, but not too heavily rock. It had to be more pop than rock if it was to capture the traditional spirit of Christmas. Now all I needed to do was come up with some suitable lyrics and a title.

I always wrote the bulk of our lyrics. Sometimes Jim would chip in a few lines to go with a particular verse or chorus that he had come up with. Once we'd finished the tune, I'd take it away and work on the words on my own for a few days. On this occasion, I wrote them all in one night. I was on one of my rare trips up to my house in Sutton Coldfield and, for some reason, I'd decided to drive over to Walsall to go to The Trumpet. It had been my local for years when I lived with my parents. It was a brilliant old jazz pub, a real spit and sawdust place. The guy who ran it in the early days was called Les Megson and it was his son, Steve, who used to make all Dave's clothes. It was only a tiny one-room pub, but it had a great atmosphere.The whole ceiling was pinned with old 78 jazz records and there were jazz photos on the wall. As usual, I was really pissed by closing time. My house was quite far away and I couldn't be bothered going back there, so I decided to go back to my mum's. I was probably too pissed to drive anyway, although there were no drink and drive laws in those days, so that never bothered anyone.

When I got to the house, both my mum and dad were in bed. I didn't feel like going to sleep, so I thought I'd start jotting down some ideas for lyrics for our Christmas single. There was no desk, I was just sitting on the bed with a pen, some paper and a bottle of Scotch. It was a terrible old bed, an ancient thing that sagged in the middle. It had been mum and dad's, but they'd bought a new one and moved theirs into my room.

I began by jotting down a list of things that people associate with Christmas. I wanted it to be about a working-class Christmas, not your picture-book snowflakes and jingle-bells job. I wrote 'Reindeer, Father Xmas, hanging up stockings, your grannies and aunties coming round for tea'. Then I started on the chorus. As soon as I got down the line, 'So here it is, Merry Xmas, everybody's having fun', I was off. I knew right away that I'd finish that night. I got into the flow of it and the rest just came really quickly. Once I'd done the chorus, I started on the first verse. I wrote, 'Are you hanging up your stocking on the wall, it's the time that every Santa has a ball'. I thought, 'What a fantastic opening line'. I just churned out the rest. I kept looking at my list and swopping all the Christmas references around. The last thing I had to do was write a lyric for the middle-eight. I looked at what words I had left on my list and came up with 'What will your daddy do when he sees your Mama kissing Santa Claus?'. That was it. It was 7am and I had finished. With other songs, I'd go back to the lyrics every couple of days and chop and change them about. With this one, I knew I didn't have to. I don't know if it had helped that I had got totally pissed, but it worked anyway. It was a very lucrative night indeed.

The next day, I took the lyrics back to Jim and he loved them. The words really made the song come alive. The pair of us then played what we'd got to the band and Chas. Everyone went mad. We had no idea how we were going to record it at that point, but we knew it would be a huge hit. We were almost certain it would go to No.1, but we never imagined it would still be going strong 25 years later. Nor could I have guessed that the very first song I had ever written would be the song we were to become most famous for.

We didn't record 'Merry Xmas Everybody' until we went out to the States. We didn't have time. We had put down a rough track of it in London when Don was still recuperating, but that was all. During the American tour, while we were in New York, we went to a studio called Record Plant to record it properly. It was the weirdest place. It was in a skyscraper building, but not a record company, just a normal office block. It took about five days to record the song. That was a long time for us. We usually spent a maximum of two days in the studio on each single. Albums only took two or three weeks. When we first thought we'd finished it, we listened back to it, but decided we didn't really like it. It was too cluttered. It had to be more bare. We didn't want it to come across as romantic. So we stripped it back down to the bare bones and rearranged it. Then we recorded it in a totally different way to how we usually worked. For the first time ever, we didn't have the band playing en masse. We layered all the different parts, starting with the drums, then the bass, then the guitars and so on until we finished with the vocals. That's the way nearly all records are made these days and it was already quite a common process back then, just one we had never used before.

Before we finished, we wanted to put our usual rowdy stamp on the song with some en masse singing and handclapping. The studio wasn't echoey enough, so we all went out into the corridor outside. We ran the mic leads right out on to the public staircase. It must have been a bizarre sight. The four of us were getting really into singing about Christmas, standing there clapping our hands, while loads of Yanks in suits were going about their business. To make matters worse, it was a boiling hot day. It was early autumn, but it was still so humid and sticky. It was absolute murder. We could hardly breathe, let alone sing. People thought we were crazy. No one asked us why we were singing about Christmas in September, they just gave us odd looks and hurried by.

We loved 'Merry Xmas' when it was finished. It captured exactly what we wanted. It was a straightforward singa-long song, much poppier and more commercial than our usual rock records, but not soppy or traditional at all. A lot of people don't realise that 'Merry Xmas Everybody' has no typical Christmassy sounds on it at all. There are no sleigh-bells or anything like that, just a few little harpsichords. The only festive thing about it is the lyrics. The song went to No.1 in France the following Easter. They didn't have a clue what it was about. They just thought it was a great pop record, which it was.

Chas was over the moon. He wouldn't stop raving about the song and how big a hit it was going to be. He flew back to England from New York specially to play it to Polydor, which was no small thing considering how much he hated flying. We hadn't even told Polydor that it was going to be a Christmas-themed record. As soon as they heard it, they flipped. They began work on a marketing strategy for it straightaway. They spent weeks planning it. They wanted to start the promotion from as soon as 'My Friend Stan' dropped out of the charts. The record was to come out a fortnight before Christmas and they wanted to make sure it went straight in at No.1. They knew that would be a hard thing to achieve at Christmas time, but they had so much confidence in it.

After the American jaunt, we played a European tour, then returned home to prepare for some UK dates over

Christmas. 'Merry Xmas Everybody' started to get played on radio a couple of weeks before release. Our fans were already going mad for it. It was the perfect festive radio record. It was also a real antidote to what was happening in the country at the time. We were right in the middle of a disastrous period politically. There were power cuts every day and half the work force seemed to be on strike. 'Merry Xmas' was a happy uplifting record. I'm sure that's part of the reason why so many people liked it.

We were presented with a silver disc for the single before it was even released. It had 500,000 pre-orders, which was phenomenal for those days. It came out on a Saturday. By Monday, it had another 300,000 re-orders. On the Tuesday morning, it went straight in at No.1. By the time Christmas came, it had sold more than a million copies. It was the fastest-selling single ever in the UK up to that point. It stayed at No.1 for a fortnight after Christmas, so it was there for a full month. Who was buying it after Christmas, I have no idea. I do know that it sent our profile through the roof. For that month, we really were the biggest thing in Britain.

When you reach the pinnacle of any profession, there's only one way to go. 'Merry Xmas Everybody' was to be our last No.1. Had anybody told us that at the time, we would never have believed them. Like all bands at the top, we thought our success would last forever. It wasn't that we suddenly fell out of favour. For the next 18 months, we were still having Top 3 hits, but we never reached the heights of 'Merry Xmas Everybody' again.

From 1974 on, a lot changed, not only for us but for all the other glam bands. It became obvious pretty quickly that glam rock was on its way out. It was inevitable. The scene had become so big so fast that the bubble had to burst. There was nowhere else glam could go. The outfits couldn't get any more outrageous and the records couldn't get any rowdier. As for the press, they were desperate to find something new to write about. There was nothing left to be said about glam. They had already turned on Bolan. His career had been in decline for six months and he was no longer having even Top 10 hits. We were at the height of our success, but we knew we had to change to make sure our career didn't go the same way.

In April, we released our first single since 'Merry Xmas Everybody'. It was a ballad called 'Everyday'. It had already come out on an album and it was a fixture of our stage show. In fact, it was one of the most popular songs in our set. That was the first time we put out a slow song as a single. It was an attempt to do something different. We'd had loads of rowdy rock hits and we'd released a few pop ditties like 'Look Wot You Dun' and 'My Friend Stan'. We had always performed ballads on stage and everyone loved them, so we thought, 'Why not get a Slade ballad in the charts?'

The original idea for 'Everyday' came from Jim's missus. She had sung the first line of it one day when he was tinkling around on the piano. I think she just hummed something, which sparked off a melody. Jim wrote the tune there and then. It was the first time one of our songs had been written on a piano, so it sounded quite unusual for us. We'd had piano parts on songs before, but this was different. The tune was driven by the piano line, not guitars. The opening verse was just me singing to a soft piano backing.

'Everyday' didn't make No.1 in Britain – it got to No.2 – but it topped the charts in loads of other countries and it was a massive stage number right until the end of Slade. One of the reasons it didn't make it as high as we'd hoped was that it had come out on the album *Old New Borrowed And Blue* which was No.1 a few months earlier. From then on, we always released singles from albums, which we had never done before. In retrospect, I think that was a mistake.

The fans loved 'Everyday', but most of them didn't understand why we had brought it out as a single.They thought it was a strange choice. They wanted us to keep making rowdy rock records, but we knew we had done all

191

we could in that department. We didn't want to keep just churning out the same sort of song. On stage and on albums, we had always done lots of different types of tracks.

We were still trying to figure out where to go next with our career, when Chas came up with one of his ideas. He said, 'I think the next step for Slade is to make a movie'. We thought it was a great idea. It would be something different for us and the fans would love it. It would also let them see a different side to Slade. We agreed immediately in principle, but insisted that we have a big say in the script. We told Chas, 'There's no way we're going to do a slapstick run-around-a-field type of film.' It had to be a proper story. None of us had ever acted before, but we didn't think there was any point in us doing a speeded-up throwaway glorified promo video.

In the spring of 1974, Chas put the feelers out for writers to come up with ideas for a script. The original movie we were going to make was a comedy. It was all Chas' assistant's idea. He was a guy called John Steel, who had been the drummer in The Animals. His film was to be called *The Quite-A-Mess Experiment*. It was a piss-take of *The Quatermass Xperiment*, a '50s sci-fi classic, and I was to be the mad professor. We all loved the idea and we were all dead keen to go ahead with it. Well, all of us except Dave. The problem was that the monster was supposed to eat Dave in the first half hour. Then we'd just leave his hair sticking out of the monster's mouth for the rest of the film. We came up with loads of daft drunken ideas like that. We had worked out the whole format and it really was very funny. I mean, I have no idea if it would have worked, but we were never to find out. Dave put his foot down. He was having none of it and there was no way anyone was going to change his mind.

Eventually, we found a script that we all agreed on. It was written by a bloke called Andrew Birkin and the storyline was based on a band called Flame. It was basically a look behind the scenes at what goes on in the music industry. No one had ever done that before. The band was to be played by the four of us, but it wasn't specifically about Slade. Flame was a fictional group. We loved the idea because it could be a mixture of our experiences and the experiences of loads of other bands that we knew – how they were ripped off, gangster connections, dodgy deals and so on. We told Andrew to go away and write the whole screenplay, but when he'd finished, we weren't happy with it. It was as though it was written by someone who knew nothing about the music business. None of the stories rang true.

We thought the best thing to do was take Andrew out on tour with us. That way, he could find out first-hand what life in a band was really like. We were due to go back to America, so we invited both him and the director, Richard Loncrane, to come along. Richard's now quite a big name in the film business, but back then, he was just starting out. Our film was to be his directorial debut. We definitely dropped him in at the deep end. The same went for Andrew. Neither of them had ever been on the road with a band before. They were supposed to come out with us for six weeks, so that while we were travelling or waiting about before shows, we could tell them all about our past and pass on stories we had heard from other bands. The pair of them only lasted two weeks. All the drinking, partying, early mornings and travelling got to them and, after a fortnight, they told us they had to go home. They hadn't realised what life on tour was going to be like. They got so stressed out by it all. We had laid it on thick for them, but only so that they could get a good feel for it. We took them out all night every night, plied them with booze, introduced them to groupies, the lot. They were shell-shocked.

The tour experience proved to be very fruitful. After Andrew returned to England, he rewrote the script and it was a million times better. It was what being in a band was really like. As soon as we gave it the green light, Chas began organising it all. He was the one who set everything up, not us. He got the finance and he persuaded David Puttnam's company, Goldcrest, to produce it. Puttnam was still in the early stages of his career, but he was definitely the up-and-coming guy as far as British films were concerned. His company had made *That'll Be The Day* with David Essex, so he already had a good idea of what making a rock film involved.

Together with Goldcrest, Chas sorted out the schedule for shooting. The whole film was to be done over six weeks in the summer. Before that, Jim and I had to come up with some songs for the soundtrack. There had to be a lot of music in the movie anyway and we wanted to capitalise on that by bringing an album out to tie in with it. We wrote twelve songs that fitted into a rough copy of the screenplay. They were in a Slade vein, but they were written for the fictional band Flame. All of the tracks had elements of our sound in them. We didn't want it to seem as though the band on screen was just us under a different name, but it was still our music and we had to play it.

The first song we wrote for the film became the first single. It was called 'Far Far Away'. The plan was to pre-empt the movie, to let people know it was on its way. We also thought it would help if the soundtrack included a couple of songs which had already been hits. I had written the bulk of 'Far Far Away' on our last US tour. The tune for it came to me out of the blue. It was one night after a gig in Memphis and Chas and I were getting drunk together on the balcony of his hotel room. We were standing looking out over the Mississippi, watching all the paddle-steamers go by. We had been away from home for ages and we were both feeling pretty homesick. I was talking about the things we'd seen on tour and what we'd missed back home. Then the intro of this tune just popped into my head. I started drunkenly singing it to Chas. Straight away, he said, 'Go to your room now and write that down. Try and finish it tonight, while you're on a roll.' That was typical of Chas. He never switched off. That night, I wrote all the verses and most of the chorus to 'Far Far Away'. The song was originally intended to be just a regular Slade single, but it ended up as one of the main tracks on the movie.

'Far Far Away' is probably my favourite ever Slade song. When it came out, it got to No.2, so it wasn't one of our biggest hits, but like 'Everyday', it's one of the songs people remember us most for. It stood out because it wasn't like our usual rocky singles. 'Far Far Away' has been used as the music in adverts all over the world ever since it was released, because it has such a distinctive melody. The German equivalent of the Co-op used it just last year and it became a hit there all over again.

With the songs for the film written and recorded we could get down to shooting. We had six weeks and no longer. We were due back in the States after that, so there was no way the schedule could overrun. While Jim and I had been away working on the music, Chas and the team had come up with a title for the film – it was to be called *Slade In Flame*. They had also cast all the other parts. We ended up with some great actors. Tom Conti played one of the band's managers. It was his first film role. No one had heard of him before. We had a guy called Ken Colley, who is now quite a well-known actor, and Johnny Shannon who was in *Performance* with Mick Jagger. Johnny played Flame's first gangster-crook manager. He was so good that he was given almost exactly the same part in loads of movies after that. He's from the East End of London and used to train boxers, so he was a bit of a hardcase in real life. He was perfect for the role. Tom Conti played Flame's second manager. He took over from Johnny when the band became successful. He wasn't a music industry person though. He was a guy who sold baked beans and cornflakes and thought he could market rock music the same way. Ken played his assistant and the female lead was Sara Clee who played Dave's girlfriend.

Another of the main roles was played by Alan Lake, who was then Diana Dors' husband. He was a well-known character in acting circles in the '70s, but he was also a notorious nutter. When we started shooting, he had not long come out of jail. He had been sent down with the singer Leapy Lee, who had a hit in the '60s with a song called 'Little Arrows'. Alan Lake was a fantastic character, but he was mad, no doubt about it. It was always the drink that got him into trouble. He played the original singer in the band that was to become Flame. I wasn't in the band at the start of the movie. It was Jim, Dave and Don and Alan. I was in another band called The Undertakers. Then Alan Lake gets the shove from Flame and I replace him.

Filming was bloody hard work, particularly for the four of us, because we had never acted before. We were up at 6am every morning and on set for 7am. A lot of the scenes were shot on location in towns all over the country. In the first couple of weeks, we were in London, Sheffield and Brighton. On the first day, we filmed at a little club in Mayfair. In the script, it was supposed to be a rock venue, but in fact it was a strip club.I was on set, although I wasn't actually in any of the scenes. It was an Alan Lake day. In fact, it was almost Alan Lake's only day. By mid-afternoon, Chas had fired him.

We hadn't really met Alan before, except for a few brief meetings, but we got on great with him. The morning shoot went fine, but come lunchtime, he went out on the piss. When he came back in the afternoon, he set about the club manager – the real one, not the one in the film. He picked a fight with him. I have no idea what it was about, nothing probably. Alan was just that type of guy. When he had a few drinks inside him, anything could spark him off. His eyes would just glaze over and he'd go mad for no reason. When he was sober, he was nice as pie, really witty and charismatic. Chas said straight away that he had to go. We couldn't risk him holding us back every day because the schedule was so tight. He was fired on the spot.

That night, Diana Dors came to see us. She begged us to give Alan another chance. She said, 'I promise I'll look after him. I'll make sure he doesn't have another drink for the whole of the filming. Not while he's on set anyway.' Eventually, we agreed.We did like him and it would have been more trouble to find someone else at such short notice.

Also, he was great for the part. He was meant to be a nutcase in the film, which is precisely what he was.

Thanks to Diana's constant supervision, Alan didn't have another drink for the rest of the shoot. We were really glad we'd let him stay. Whenever we were hanging around on set, he kept us all entertained. He would tell us stories about his gangland connections, his time in jail and his mates like the Krays. After that first little upset, it all went incredibly smoothly, although it was an exhausting six weeks. When we saw the rough cuts of the film, we were delighted. Considering our lack of acting experience, we thought we had done a really good job.

Slade In Flame was quite a heavy movie. It was about fallings-out in bands and all the repercussions they cause. There was a lot of violence and it had a very downbeat ending. When it was first finished, the censors wanted to give it an X-certificate. We had to edit a good deal of the violence out to get it down to an A-certificate, which would now be a PG. We couldn't get a U-certificate without editing so much that we would have lost half the story. It was a shame for some of our younger fans, who couldn't get in to see it, but we wanted it to be taken seriously, so there was nothing else we could do. Even after it was watered down, it was still a very dark unsettling film. People were shocked by it.

The great thing about *Slade In Flame* was that it showed things that go on behind the scenes in rock bands, things that punters then knew nothing about. Today, there's so much interest in pop music that most of that stuff is common knowledge. The industry itself has changed a lot too. It's much more regulated now. The film was specifically set in the late '60s rather than the '70s – everyone dressed in '60s fashions – because that was when most of the real dodgy dealings went on. Even by the mid '70s, the music business had cleaned up its act a hell of a lot, but there's still a long way to go.

When we had the premiere in London, members of the fan club and the general public were downstairs and up in the balcony, it was all industry people. The two groups were laughing at completely different bits. The insiders knew exactly what we were getting at and who a lot of the characters were based on. The public didn't have a clue. The best bits probably passed them by.

The four of us arrived at the premiere on a fire engine. It was our publicist's idea, a stunt to get some extra press. It tied in with the film quite nicely though. Flame get involved in all sorts of mad situations in the movie. It was just the sort of thing they'd do. The screening was at a big cinema by Victoria Station. It was a real showbizzy event. The whole cast was there, including Alan Lake and Tom Conti, plus loads of other actors and film industry people. Just about every big '70s band who could make it turned up – Suzi, Thin Lizzy, Sweet, everyone. A lot of them had given us ideas for the script, although not intentionally. Some of the stories were things that had happened to us, others were based on tales we had heard over the years.

My first scene in the film is our version of something that happened to Screaming Lord Sutch. I'm not in Flame at this point. I'm the singer in another band, The Undertakers. We're on stage and I'm wearing a real macabre outfit – a big black cloak and hat – with ghoulish white make-up on my face. It gets to a part of the show where I'm supposed to appear from a coffin after a big explosion. In the film, Alan Lake's character has nailed the lid of the coffin shut and I can't get out. We got that story from one of our roadies, Haden, who used to work with Screaming Lord Sutch. It was one of Sutch's regular stunts. One night, a new member of the crew took the coffin on stage. He accidentally propped it up against the wall the wrong way round. During the gig, there was a big explosion, then nothing happened. Everyone was waiting for Screaming Lord Sutch to climb out of this coffin. But he couldn't because the lid was right against the wall. No big entrance that night.

Another scene in the film showed us on the ship of a pirate radio station. In the '60s, pirate stations were a big deal. All bands did interviews with them. They were on boats moored way off the coast, because they had to stay outside certain limits to be able to broadcast. We'd heard a story about the owner of one pirate station being shot by gangsters in London. It was a sort of turf war about who could broadcast from where. In the film, Flame go to do promotion at a pirate station on a boat moored miles out in the Thames Estuary. Tommy Vance played the DJ. While we're doing our interview, a boat goes past and fires a machine gun at the station. The scene was shot on what was basically an old look-out post way out to sea. The four of us had to climb on to it, then up ladders at the sides. It was terrible weather that day. There was a gale-force wind and the sea was really choppy. It was pretty scary, not to mention bloody dangerous. In the end, we had to be lifted off by helicopter, because that was easier than getting us back on the boat. Dave hated it. It wasn't his thing at all. He almost fell off the ladder into the sea a couple of times.

When *Slade In Flame* came out, it got a mixed reception. The critics loved it. Even the big critics from the serious papers gave it great reviews. That amazed us. We had expected them to slate it. The public weren't so sure. Our fans liked it because we were in it, but they were shocked by it. It wasn't what they wanted from us. They had expected a fun lighthearted film. It did have a lot of laughs in it, but it wasn't all jolly. I don't think many of them could understand why we had made parts of it so heavy. In the movie, as soon as Flame become successful, the band members start rowing and fighting. Then they split up. It's a very sad and low-key ending.

Today, more people get what the film is about. It's regularly cited as one of the best rock movies ever made. The National Film Theatre in London have a screening of it almost every year. Whenever it's on, they ask me to come along and give a lecture. I was never able to do it until last year. They were showing it on a Saturday night and I wasn't working, so I agreed to go and do a talk beforehand. I was a bit apprehensive, because I'd never done anything like that before. I hadn't seen the film for nearly twenty years either, certainly not on a big screen. When I got up to talk before the screening, I had no idea what I was going to say. I hadn't planned anything. I wanted to see what the audience was like first. I couldn't believe it. The place erupted as soon as I walked on stage. The crowd just went crazy.

I said a few words about making the film, then I sat in the audience to watch it. I'd forgotten how heavy it was. At the end, everyone was applauding and standing up. I had to go back on stage for a question and answer session. It was supposed to last twenty minutes. Two hours later, I was still there. I was really chuffed at how well it had stood up. The public rate it a lot better now, because they understand more of what the pop business is about.

Just after *Slade In Flame* was released, we brought out the main theme as a single. It was called 'How Does It Feel'. It was used as incidental music throughout the film and it played over the credits. It was a hit, but not a huge success – it only reached No.11 – although it's now cited as one of our finest songs. It just didn't work that well as a pop single in its own right. It had a very cinematic sound and we used a brass section on it, which was the first time we'd done that.

The good reaction from the critics led to us being immediately inundated with other offers. The only one we were interested in was with Ronnie Barker and Ronnie Corbert. It was to be a spoof spy comedy and we were to play a pop group. The story was that a top-secret film gets smuggled into the country, hidden in our equipment. Lots of people are chasing us to get it back. I don't think it was ever made, although it was a great script. We turned it down because we couldn't afford to take any more time out of our career. All in all, the film and the soundtrack and the subsequent promotion had cost us a year. We had to get back to recording and touring as Slade.

By the start of 1975, we were in much the same position as we had been in at the start of 1974, in that we still weren't

sure where to take our career next. The film had been a
diversion, but it hadn't left us with any future plans. We
had to make a conscious decision. None of us wanted to
keep plodding along doing what we had done for years –
releasing an album, going on tour, then releasing another
album . . . The only market we hadn't cracked properly was
the States, so we decided to up sticks and move over there
properly for eighteen months. We did one last tour of
Europe, then headed for New York. We planned to come
back occasionally to plug singles and do the odd TV show,
but all our recording and touring was to be done over there.

Moving to America was like a fresh start for us, a new
challenge. It kept us going. We were fed up of doing the
same circuit in Europe and Asia. We based ourselves in
New York, although most of the time we were touring all
over the country. I booked into a big suite at The Mayflower
Hotel and the other three got apartments. We really got to
know New York for the first time and I loved it. There were
great clubs and always gigs to go to. We met some fantastic
people too.

When we'd been over there for about six months, Dave
and Jim invited their wives to come out for a holiday.
Dave's wife had just had a kid before we left and he was
desperate to see her. I asked my girlfriend over to stay with
me. She was called Leandra. We'd known each other for a
couple of years, but we'd only really got together when we
were making the film. I had met her through Swin. If I ever
went out with someone from the band's circle, it was
usually with Swin or Don. Swin had been seeing a girl in
London called Sandy, who worked at Olympic Studios, and
once when I went with him to her house, I met Leandra. She
and Sandy were best friends and they later became
flatmates. Leandra didn't like me at all when we first met.
She was a dress designer and she was into cooler singers
like Bowie and Bolan. She thought we were a bunch of
scraggy yobbos and she hated our music. When we
eventually got talking, we found out that we got on quite
well and started to see one another very casually. Then

when we were making the film, we hung out together all the time because I was based in London.

Leandra flew over to New York with Dave and Jim's wives. At first, none of them wanted to come. They thought it was too dangerous. They said, 'We've heard what it's like over there. It's not safe to walk down the street. We'll wait until you're in another city, then we'll come and visit.' We said, 'Don't be so bloody ridiculous. That's all hype. There's no more trouble here than there is back home.' We'd never once had a problem in New York and we thought we knew the place pretty well after six months of living there.

On the first day that the girls arrived, they went to a bank to change some money. You wouldn't believe it, but two minutes after they'd walked in, the place was held up. A gunman charged in, then ordered them all to lie face down on the floor, just like in the movies. Dave's missus had their little kid with her. The police turned up and there was a shoot-out. The woman lying next to Leandra on the floor was hit by a bullet. It was from one of the cops. It ricocheted off the wall and went into her. Leandra and the others weren't hurt, but they were terrified. It took them days to get over it. We had been out of town at a gig that day, and when we got back to the hotel, we found them all sitting in the bar, shaking. They started screaming at us. They were going, 'We told you this would happen. We said this was a dangerous place. You know nothing about New York.' They couldn't wait to get home.

Between tours, we worked on a new album. We recorded it at Record Plant in New York, which was where we had made 'Merry Xmas Everybody'. We were sharing the studio with John Lennon. We had it during the day, then he would come in at night. After we'd left, Chas used to stay on to do some mixing until Lennon arrived. Chas knew him quite well anyway. Chas knew everyone. One night, Lennon came in when Chas was listening back to one of our tracks. Apparently, Lennon said, 'Who is this? I love the bloke's voice. He sounds just like me.' Lots of people had said I sounded like Lennon before, but I never thought so.

When I heard that Lennon had said it himself, I was over the moon. It was one of the best compliments I ever got, even though I wasn't there to hear it.

We called the album *Nobody's Fool*. It was very different from anything we had done before. It had quite a soulful sound, although it was a real mixture of tracks. On some, we used black girl backing singers and a brass section. A lot of the songs were influenced by the music we had been hearing on the radio while we were over there. I thought it was a good album and I still enjoy it, but it wasn't hugely successful back home. It wasn't rocky and that's what our fans wanted to hear.

The single 'Nobody's Fool' came out in Britain in April 1976. We flew back from the States a couple of times to do promotion and I always stayed with Leandra in London. On one of those trips, she got pregnant. We didn't find out until I was back in New York. She phoned to tell me. I thought it was great. It was bad timing because I couldn't get home to see her, but there was never going to be a good time. That's just how it is when you're in a working band and we both knew that.

We came back to Britain briefly in the middle of 1976. We still hadn't cracked the States, not nationally anyway. We had resigned ourselves to the fact that certain cities weren't ready for us. We hadn't given up hope though. We were sure we would break through eventually, when the time was right. In America, tastes don't change every couple of years like they do over here. It takes a lot longer, because the place is so vast. We had made progress and we were prepared to keep at it.

Leandra and I got married towards the end of August. It was a blazing hot summer that year and this was a particularly killer-hot day. Apart from our parents, we didn't tell anyone what we were planning until the day before. I wanted to keep it a secret to avoid the press. It was all done very quickly and quietly. We were married at lunchtime in a registry office in Lichfield. The only guests were our families, the band and a few friends. The band were mad that I hadn't told them about it earlier, but they couldn't really complain. None of them had told me when they were planning to get married. I hadn't even been invited to their weddings. I reminded them about that. I said, 'How much notice did you guys give me?' That shut them up.

My best man was Swin. Later, when he got married, I was his best man. I remember the pair of us had three or four whiskys before we set off for the registry office, so we were both a bit pissed when we got there. It was a fantastic day, really sunny, but so hot. Two friends of ours, Alan and Wendy, a couple who lived in the Midlands, put on the reception. They had a huge house and they just threw a big party. Everyone knew that Leandra was pregnant. By the time we got married, she was five months gone. I dare say her parents weren't thrilled about that, but it didn't seem to bother them too much. I had known them for years and they liked me. They were a bit wary of me at first, largely because I was in a band. But Leandra had always hung around with musicians. She designed clothes for quite a few groups.

The day after the wedding, I had to drive down to London. We were mixing some new songs. The studio was booked and we were only back in Britain for a short time, so we couldn't cancel it. There wasn't any time for a honeymoon. Leandra wasn't keen to travel then anyway because she was so pregnant. She was already really big and it was blistering hot all over Europe. I think she was happier to stay at home. Much later, we went away to Paris for a week, but we never had a proper honeymoon.

Our first kid, Charisse, was born on December 27th. She was due to arrive on Christmas day, but she came two days late. I didn't have a drink the whole of that Christmas just in case I had to drive Leandra to the hospital. We chose the name Charisse after the Hollywood movie dancer Cyd Charisse because Leandra said she did so much kicking in the womb. We were living in London then, in a big flat by the river in Chelsea. I still had my house in the Midlands and we sometimes went there at weekends. During the week, I was usually recording in London, if I wasn't away on tour.

In 1977, we moved back permanently from the States. While we had been away, the whole punk explosion had happened in Britain. We knew it had been going on, because we had been following it in the music press, but we didn't realise how big an impact it was going to have on our career. Our status totally changed. We were still getting hits, particularly in Europe, but they were just about Top 10s, no longer No.1s or top 3s. Punk sent bands like us out of favour. Everyone thought our day was over.

WHATEVER

HAPPENED

TO . . .

10

While we were away in the States, someone had written 'Whatever happened to Slade' in huge letters along the side of one of the Thames bridges. It was quite a famous piece of graffiti. It was there for years. We went to see it and we all loved it. We had recorded a second album in New York and it was due for release. We wanted to call it *Whatever Happened To Slade* and use a shot of the bridge on the sleeve. The record company liked the title, but not the cover idea. In the end, they used a photo of the four of us standing side by side in a street. There were four poster hoardings on a wall above our heads and in them were four pictures of us in our skinhead days.

Whatever Happened To Slade was much rockier than *Nobody's Fool*. It was a return to our original sound. We did a British tour to promote it, which sold out, because they were our first shows there for two years. We were probably a better live band than we had been before we went away. In America, we couldn't rely on the name Slade to impress an audience, so we had worked hard on improving our music and our playing.

We continued to write and record, but we had stopped getting any big hits. The problem was that we couldn't get our songs played on the radio. We were considered old hat. We had to decide whether to carry on or call it a day. We all had to agree one way or the other. We sat down and talked about it. We wanted to go on. We thought, 'We're still filling big venues, still making what we consider good records. Let's stay together and see how it goes.' It wasn't as though we weren't making any money. We were doing okay. A lot of other bands would have been happy with the success we were getting. Our sales were only disappointing by our own standards. We were used to being one of the biggest bands in the world. It was inevitable that we couldn't stay at that level. It happens to every band. You have to drop back. You reach your peak, then you have to settle on a lower plateau. I'm sure that if we had been making shit records, we would have admitted it to ourselves and thrown in the towel. We knew we could still produce good material. It was just that it wasn't right for that time.

By 1978, we had basically gone back to square one. We were taking gigs anywhere and everywhere. We still played the occasional concert hall, but we were also doing universities, theatres and even clubs. We always went down well, if only because we had a lot of old hits that people still loved to hear. We weren't just doing a nostalgia show though. We were determined not to fall into that. We were doing our new material too, which was going down okay.

Through 1978 and 1979, our hits petered off and our radio play dried up. We were even doing gigs at glorified cabaret clubs. We'd take all the equipment in there and put on a proper rock show. In some venues, they'd had the likes of Little and Large on the week before. It did feel strange playing places like that, but we had made a conscious decision to carry on and we couldn't fill concert halls anymore, so there was no alternative. We just told ourselves that at some point, if we put out the right record at the right time, we could break through again. In our heart of hearts, we truly believed that.

Europe helped to keep us going. We were still selling out quite big venues over there. We did a tour of Poland which was all arenas, mainly outdoor places. One was an arena Hitler had built for his Nazi rallies. The only bands from the West who had played in Poland before us were Procol Harum and Abba, but they had only done one-off shows in

Warsaw. No Western bands had toured there. We went over in 1979. While we were there, the Pope died. I remember it really well because the whole country was in mourning. The other thing I'll never forget about Poland was the food. It was awful, truly inedible. Everywhere we went, we were given this chicken soup which had a thick layer of fat over the top. There was no chicken in it at all. It was just broth and giblets. The Poles reckoned that eating it helped to keep them warm. They also told us to have a shot of vodka after each meal. Apparently, it helped kill off the harmful bacteria in the food.

All four of us spent the whole of that tour with the shits. Every night on stage, we'd be running off one at a time in front of vast audiences to go to the bog. It was the same for our crew. The funniest night was when our soundman, Charlie, got the shits really bad. He was up at the desk in the middle of the crowd and he couldn't leave until the end of the show. He had to shit himself in the sound booth. Someone got a message through to us on stage about what had happened. It was hysterical. We could see Charlie at the desk. The look on his face was classic. We could hardly play for laughing.

For most of our career we played 'Mama Weer All Crazee Now' as the first song in our encores. Backstage, we always had piles and piles of toilet rolls. When we started the song, the crew would throw all these toilet rolls out into the audience. They'd unravel like they were huge streamers. We got through literally hundreds of them every night. The punters would catch them and throw them back at us. They'd be going backwards and forwards from the stage, unravelling more and more. It was brilliant. It made for a real party carnival atmosphere. In Poland, as we soon found out, toilet rolls were like luxuries. At our first gig there, they were all thrown out into the crowd as usual. We were waiting for them to come back. And waiting. . . Nothing. The punters just picked them up and kept them. They were hiding them in their coats. Apparently, toilet rolls were so scarce that people had to queue for ages for them. There was no way anyone was going to throw theirs back on stage.

Back in Britain, our luck didn't look like it was ever going to change. We were playing places like Baileys in Watford. We could fill that sort of venue for seven nights on the trot. It was a fair number of punters over a week, but it wasn't the sort of place people associated us with. I didn't mind too much. Obviously, it wasn't ideal, but I didn't find it depressing. I was still playing, still writing, still getting new ideas. None of us was enamoured with our situation, but at least while we were actually on stage, we enjoyed ourselves.

We had stopped wearing glam-style gear like the platform boots even before we went to live in the States – our look was less over the top. Punks hated all the older bands. In fact, they hated everything. That was what they said in the press anyway. The truth was that a lot of the big punk bands used to come to our gigs. We played Camden Palace in London quite a lot and the likes of Bob Geldof and The Damned were always in the audience. Geldof was a big Slade fan. He'd come into our dressing room after the show to talk to us. I remember him saying, 'I'd never do what you guys are doing. I'd never go back to playing little venues like this. You must be mad.' And what happened? Five years later, The Boomtown Rats were doing exactly the same thing. Many bands go through it at some time in their career. They have to, at least they do if they don't split up.

It was funny, because most of the musicians who slagged us off in the papers were nice as pie when we met them. They'd say, 'You're the reason I started singing' or 'I took up the guitar when I heard one of your records.' The Stranglers loved us. They told us they used to have 'Gudbuy T' Jane' in their set. They couldn't admit to that in public. It was the punk way to rubbish everyone. We understood that. We were a lot smarter about the industry than they were. The young bands didn't know the score, because it was all new to them. They were riding high in the charts back then and they thought it was going to last forever. We had thought the same when we were in their position. Every act does. In the end, most of the punk bands died off far quicker than we did. The '70s survivors, people like Elton John and Rod Stewart, had hardly any hits in Britain in the '80s. They had to wait a long time to come back into fashion.

After two years of being back on the club and ballroom circuit, we began to feel like we were on a hiding to nothing. We still weren't getting any radio play. Without that, we couldn't get back to bigger venues. It was only at Christmas that we could fill large-sized places like Hammersmith Odeon. Another problem was that we weren't making much money. We weren't selling many records and we had never earned a lot from touring. By the end of 1979, Jim and I were propping up the band from our writing royalties. The pair of us were better off than Dave and Don, because we were still making money from the old hits.

None of us could see any light at the end of the tunnel. The best we could manage was the occasional minor hits and the odd appearance on *Top Of The Pops*. Most of our records got nowhere near the Top 20. We had no idea how to get out of our situation either. It was the first time we had come up against it. It was the same for Chas. Both acts he had been involved with before – The Animals and Hendrix – had finished at the height of their success. We had looked to Chas for a plan, but he was as puzzled as we were.

Matters came to a head one day. Chas had called Jim and me into his office. He wasn't trying to be malicious, but he said, 'I think Slade should call it a day as a four-piece. I think you and Jim should break away from the others and form a new group.' I definitely wasn't into the idea. I said, 'No way, Chas. I'll never do that.' There was no point in it anyway. I said, 'If I'm going to leave the others, I may as well go solo. I'm not starting another band.' I'd had tons of offers to make solo albums all the way through the '70s, but I'd never done it because of my loyalty to Slade. I didn't want to be a solo act if Slade was still going.

That was the first nail in the coffin of our relationship

with Chas. It was a shame because we hadn't had any major rows, but in my mind, for him even to make that suggestion wasn't right. I was probably closer to Chas than anyone else in the band, but still I went straight to Dave and Don to tell them what he had said. I had to. There was no way I could keep something like that from them. At the end of the day, I owed even more loyalty to them than I did to Chas.

As you can imagine, Dave and Don didn't take the news too well. Dave was already pretty low anyway and wavering about what to do next. By then, we had more or less stopped performing and recording. None of us ever said, 'Slade is finished,' but it just petered out. Jim started doing some solo recording. He had a makeshift band with his brother called The Dummies and they put a single out. Dave didn't seem at all interested in carrying on. Don would have done, but he wasn't bothered either way. It really did seem to be the end.

The one good thing that came out of the demise of the band, at least as far as I was concerned, was that I could finally spend some time with my family – my second daughter, Jessica, had been born in 1978. Although we hadn't been touring nearly as much as we did in the past, I had still missed a lot of the kids' early years. It was a drag, but it couldn't be helped. It's just something you have to accept when you make your living from a band. Leandra now persuaded me to move out of London. She wanted the kids to go to school in the Midlands. We sold the house in Sutton Coldfield and Leandra didn't like living in that area on her own anyway. She felt isolated. I was always on tour and she had no friends around there. Most of the people she knew were in Wolverhampton and that was more than thirty minutes' drive away.

I told Leandra to go and look for a house that she liked and she did. She found a lovely place on the outskirts of Wolverhampton, out in the countryside. I was quite enjoying having some time off and taking it easy when an offer came through to do the Reading Festival. It was the summer of 1980. We had asked to play Reading two years earlier, but the promoters weren't interested. That year, Whitesnake were headlining and Ozzy Osbourne was supposed to be second on the bill. He had left Black Sabbath and was forming his new band, Blizzard Of Ozz. The trouble was that they weren't ready yet, so Ozzy had pulled out of Reading with only two days to go. The organisers asked us to step in at the last minute. They couldn't get anyone else at such short notice.

We had more or less wound Slade down by this point. We had fulfilled all our contracts for recording and touring and we had let all our crew go. We hadn't done a proper gig for months. It was Chas who told us about the offer. He said, 'I know you're not really playing anymore, but I think you should do it.' I was all for it, but I didn't think for a minute Dave would agree. Chas wouldn't be put off. He was really keen. He kept saying, 'How do we talk him round? What can we say to convince him?' I went to see Dave. I told him the rest of us wanted to do it. He said, 'No way. I don't want any more to do with Slade.' As usual, Chas wasn't prepared to take no for an answer. He decided he was going to go up to Wolverhampton to have a word with Dave himself. I don't know how, but Chas talked him into it. I think more or less what he said was, 'Do this one show. If you're great or you die on your arse, it doesn't matter. Instead of Slade petering out, end on a high at a festival.' So Dave was in.

We had one rehearsal on the day before the show, just to get ourselves back into gear. It was like riding a bike. We only had to play the songs once to get back to how we had been. We'd been together for fifteen years, so it didn't take much. When we arrived at Reading, we had no backstage passes for the band. We got to the venue, parked in the public car park, then unloaded our guitars and walked through the crowd to the backstage carrying our own cases. Fortunately, we knew all the security guys because most of them had worked for us in the past, so they just let us in.

Tommy Vance was the DJ at Reading that day. We knew

him from appearing in our film and from Radio 1. When we were changing in our caravan, he came in and said, 'I think you guys will go down a storm today. This festival has been really dull so far. I'm certain you'll tear it apart. You're the only band with any songs the whole crowd can sing.'

We went on third from the top of the bill. Def Leppard were supposed to be on before us, but they insisted on being moved to above us. As it turned out, our new slot was perfect. It was twilight. As soon as we started, the crowd went crazy. We couldn't believe it. We really did tear the place apart. The reaction was incredible because a lot of that audience had never seen us before. They were too young. Even the media people down the front were getting into it and they had ignored us for years.

We played a mixture of old hits and new material and it all went down well. The crowd kept calling us back for encore after encore. We even got them singing 'Merry Xmas Everybody' in the middle of the summer. People kept shouting for it so we ended the show with it. When we came off stage, everyone was raving about our perform-ance. We were amazed. The best bit was when I walked into our caravan backstage. I was already on a high from the show. I wandered in and there was Britt Ekland. She was just sitting there. If Britt Ekland wants to hang out with you, you know you're a success. All the press and record company people who hadn't bothered with us for four years packed into the caravan. They were all congratulating us and saying how much they enjoyed the show.

Reading was one of those days that marks a complete turning point in your life. It resurrected our career. The following week, we were on the front pages of all the music papers. It was exactly what had happened at the Lincoln Festival all those years ago. We were up and running again. We wanted to bring an album out pretty much straight away. First, we had some serious business matters to sort out.

Our relationship with Chas had been going downhill for some time. I was still talking to him, but there was a very frosty atmosphere between him and Dave and Don. Dave in particular never really forgave Chas for his suggestion of getting rid of him and Don. They got on a bit better when all the dust had settled over that episode, but a lot of trust had been lost. There was also friction between Jim and Chas. Jim and his brother, Frank, had formed an independent label with Chas, called Cheapskate, to release their own recordings. They were all having rucks about it. I don't know the ins and outs of their deal, but certainly Jimmy and Frank felt that Chas wasn't treating them right. That situation got worse and worse. It was incredibly strained between the three of them. Eventually, they had a big bust-up and Chas and Jim stopped talking completely.

Even I had my doubts about Chas, although I still had a lot of allegiance to him. When we had stopped touring at the start of 1980, it was left to me to sack our whole crew. We had obviously scaled down the number of people working with us, but we still had a core of four of five people who we'd kept on retainer. They had all been with us throughout the '70s. The likes of Swin and Charlie, our sound guy, were as much a part of the band as anyone. Swin was also my best mate. We couldn't afford to keep paying them and since we weren't planning any more gigs, we had to let them go. I was annoyed that it had been left to me to do the dirty work, but then it usually was.

Another problem was that, in the late '70s, Chas had persuaded us to sign to his own label, Barn Records. He then licensed that to Polydor. It was a bit of business acumen on Chas' part. He wanted to sign other acts to Barn Records, but he needed finance from a major label. Polydor gave him money on the strength of our name. Without at least one big act, they wouldn't have been interested. We didn't realise any of this at the time, but it all came out in the wash later. For us, it was just a move of label.

Shortly after Reading, the others decided that they didn't want Chas to manage us anymore. Jim didn't want him to produce our records either. He had been taking a bit of a backseat on the production side and working with some new artists. Naturally, I had to tell Chas – the dirty work, again! But even I knew that you didn't tell Chas such things easily.

I phoned Chas up and told him that I wanted to meet. I could tell by his tone on the phone that he thought I was going to quit the band. He knew I had been getting solo offers. A few times, he'd even tried to stop me hearing about them, so that I wouldn't leave. He said, 'You're all coming to see me?' I said, 'No, Chas, just me.' So I went to his office in London. It was horrible. He knew there was something serious up as soon as I walked through the door. I was a bit wary, because he was a heavy dude when he lost his temper and I'd had stand-up rows with him several times before. It was always forgotten the next day though and we were still what I would call good friends. I said, 'I might as well come out straight and tell you, we don't want you to manage us anymore.' Chas didn't say a word. He knew it was the end of the line. He didn't even try to talk us out of it, which was very unusual for him. He never gave in without a fight. I said, 'I don't think it's working anymore. We've had enough and there's no changing our minds.'

To give Chas his due, he did do us a big favour before we split with him. As a goodwill gesture, he organised a deal with us for RCA, who had already asked to sign us. He could have insisted we stay on his label, but he didn't. He got us a really good deal too. It was good of him. Almost immediately, we brought out a single and an album, both called *We'll Bring The House Down*. The single got lots of radio play and was a big hit in Britain and massive all over Europe. It was a very rocky raucous song, an old Slade-style anthem.

In the summer of 1981, we were asked to play at the Monsters Of Rock Festival at Castle Donington. AC/DC were headlining. We got exactly the same reaction that we had at Reading. The crowd adored us. Afterwards, we brought out another single called 'Lock Up Your Daughters'. It went into the charts in Britain and Top 3 in Europe. By then, a new wave of metal bands were becoming huge, both here and in the States. Suddenly, our rowdy anthem-type rock was back in. Although we played heavy rock, not really metal, we were attracting a whole new audience of metal fans, both here and in Europe.

We weren't getting constant hits, but we were doing pretty well. We even started playing concert tours all over again. Our first tour was a great success. We opened the show with a real uptempo headbanging song called 'Rock'n'Roll Preacher'. It was the first track on the album *Til Death Do Us Part*, which also had 'Lock Up Your Daughters' on it. At the time, my stage outfit was a long dark frock-coat and flat black Spanish-style hat. I basically looked like a preacher. Our set was all stained glass, church windows with lights shining through so that they looked like sunbeams. When we played the song, we performed a mock wedding ceremony. I would walk on in my preacher's gear and say, 'Ladies and gentlemen, we are gathered here today to bring together this rock and this roll.' It freaked the audience out. After the sermon, there was thunder and lightning.

Really, I was just resurrecting the vicar stunt I had used in the '60s. I had always said I was going to bring it back. We never threw away our tricks. We just updated them. We didn't like using lots of pyrotechnics. Our effects were much simpler. Mainly, I would put the shows and the lighting ideas together. When we rehearsed, I'd sit out front with the lighting and sound guys and try to figure out what would work. It was the overall stage presence that was one of our trademarks. The idea was to keep the audience's eyes fixed to the stage. It kept people entertained.

Everything started to snowball for us again. We brought out another album, a really rocky record called *The Amazing Kamikaze Syndrome*. Then, in 1983, an American band called Quiet Riot covered 'Cum On Feel The Noize'. At first, it was just on their album. Then they put it out as a single. It sounded almost exactly like our version, a carbon copy. Ten years before, when we had released the song, it had barely dented the American charts. Quiet Riot had a massive hit with it. On the back of the success of that song, their album sold seven million copies. No one had ever heard of them before. Suddenly, on top of our new success back home, America was interested. We were getting calls from labels out there, asking us to send over our new material. It was amazing. We hadn't even been there for six years.

Towards the end of 1983, we decided to release another Christmas single. It wasn't going to be about Christmas this time, just aimed at that market. Jim came up with the perfect song. He had always wanted to write a track with a Sailing-style melody, so that's what he did. I went away and wrote lyrics and we called it 'My Oh My'. We recorded a rough version in a little demo studio off Tottenham Court Road which I owned. It was just me singing and Jim on piano. While we were in there, we put down another new song called 'Run Runaway'. That was a much rockier track, with guitars and Jim playing electric violin. It was like a rocky Scottish jig.

We took the two songs to RCA and they flipped out. They loved them and thought they could both be big hits. First though, they wanted us to record them with an outside producer. We had never done that before. It had always been either Chas or ourselves. We agreed and they brought in a guy called John Punter, who had engineered a lot of Roxy Music and Queen records. He loved 'My Oh My' and we started work on that straight away. He made us record all our parts separately, which we weren't used to.

'My Oh My' came out just before Christmas. We knew it was going to be big, because it was on the radio all the time. It was destined to be a No.1. That would have been great – two Slade singles topping the Christmas charts exactly a decade apart. No band had ever done that. In the end, it got to No.2. We were pipped to the post by the Flying Pickets. 'My Oh My' stayed at No.2 for weeks and it was No.1 all over Europe. It put the seal on our '80s career. It was followed by 'Run Runaway', another Top 10 smash. Slade was back in business.

After the Quiet Riot hit, we had signed to CBS in America. They had released *The Amazing Kamikaze Syndrome*, but with a different title. It had done okay and CBS were keen to keep working with us. When they heard our two new songs, they went mad for them. They particularly liked 'Run Runaway', because it was really rocky. They wanted to release that first, then 'My Oh My' afterwards. We had been making videos for singles since the late '70s, but we had never spent much money on them. Because 'Run Runaway' had a very Celtic feel, we filmed it in a castle. We had pipers on the parapets and everything. The Yanks loved it. It was on MTV non-stop. Even though we hadn't been to the States for years, 'Run Runaway' became a huge hit. It was Top 10 on the Billboard chart – our first American Top 10. The timing was right. Glam metal was all the rage and their bands were dressing up just as we had in the early '70s.

Since Chas' departure, we had been managing ourselves. I was doing all the day-to-day stuff and Colin Newman – who had been our business affairs guy for years and is now my manager – was looking after the financial side. We had thought about replacing Chas, but we reckoned no one knew our set-up better than ourselves. Certainly I had always been very involved in budgets, tours and other aspects of our career. When we took off in America, Ozzy Osbourne's wife, Sharon, offered to manage us over there. Both she and Ozzy were old friends of mine and Ozzy was signed to CBS too. It was Sharon who saved Ozzy's life and his career after he left Black Sabbath. She had done a great job managing him – he was huge in the States.

Sharon knew the music business inside out. She had grown up with it. Her dad, Don Arden, had been an agent and manager since the '50s. He managed loads of massive bands like Electric Light Orchestra, The Move and The Small Faces. He was a real tough character. In rock circles, he was known as the Godfather. I used to go to big showbiz parties at his house in Wimbledon. Don did throw fantastic parties. It was at one of those that I first met Sharon. Ozzy we obviously knew from the Midlands. Black Sabbath were Brummies and we had played with them quite a few times when we were starting out. Ozzy became a good mate, but we didn't really get to know each other well until the '80s, because Sabbath spent most of the '70s in America.

CBS were desperate for us to tour in the States, so we took Sharon on. The first thing she did was book us as special guests on Ozzy's upcoming tour. We were supposed to be with him for six weeks. We went over and played five warm-up shows of our own first. They were in mid-sized venues in the southern States and we went down really well. Our first show with Ozzy was in San Francisco. It went fine, but when we came off stage, Jim was really ill. He had been feeling bad ever since we'd arrived in America, but we thought it was a combination of the heat and jet lag. He was incredibly tired and he couldn't eat anything. We called for a doctor. It turned out that Jim had hepatitis. There was no way he could play. We had to cancel the whole tour. I spent the next two or three weeks based in LA, doing some promotion to try and salvage something from the trip. Then we all went back to England.

That turned out to be our last ever tour. We were planning another British tour, but I didn't want to do it. I felt like we'd had enough. On our previous UK tour, we had all been arguing. It wasn't working like it did before. For a start, we couldn't take the relentless pace anymore. Also, attitudes within the band had changed with the new whiff of success. We shouldn't have had problems, because we'd been through that before, but we did. Egos were taking over. There was friction in the studio as well as on the road. I told the others that I needed a break from touring and we cancelled our plans. It wasn't that I wanted out of Slade. I had been offered TV work and I'd already turned down parts in a couple of sitcoms. I wasn't looking for other work. I was happy to keep recording with the band.

At the time, I had personal problems to cope with as well. I was in the throws of a divorce. While we were in the States, I should have been on holiday with Leandra. She had set it all up. We hadn't been away for years and she was mad that I'd cancelled it. That was the last straw for us. We didn't fall out or anything. We were just living separate lives. Even when Slade wasn't touring, I had been managing the band and that had taken up most of my time.

On top of everything, Jim was seeing a psychiatrist, Dave became a Jehovah's Witness, and Don was drinking heavily.

Don knew he had a problem. He eventually gave up alcohol completely – he hasn't had a drink for ten years now. When he first tried to quit , he and Ozzy went to AA meetings together. Ozzy's taken every drink and drug known to man. He was a terror in his Black Sabbath days. In the '80s, he hung out in London quite a lot and Don and I saw him all the time. The three of us were drinking buddies. He and Don went to AA meetings at lunchtimes now and again. At 2.30pm, Ozzy would look at his watch, then say he had to go because the pubs were shutting in half an hour. Ozzy's been in and out of drying-out clinics. He was a real piss-head, no doubt about it. I've seen Ozzy take a pint glass, walk past all the optics behind a bar and fill it up with a mix of every different type of spirit. Then he'd knock it back and start again.

Ozzy was always great fun to go out with, because he's so sharp and witty. He never cared what he said to anyone either, which was very amusing but quite often got him into trouble. One afternoon, Ozzy and I went on a bender. He was going to see Iron Maiden that night at Hammersmith Odeon, as it was called then. He asked me to go with him. Then he said, 'We have to get something special to wear to the gig.' I'm like, 'What are you on about, Ozzy?' He dragged me into an antique shop across the road. It sold old guns and war memorabilia. We were both really pissed by this point. Ozzy bought a German war helmet. He said, 'I'm going to wear this tonight.' I said, 'No, you're not.' But, of course, he did. Worse still, we then went to a fancy dress shop and hired both of us ballerina costumes. We had to go to the Iron Maiden gig in them, with him in his helmet too.

There's no arguing with Ozzy when he makes up his mind to do something. You get sucked in.

I remember we stood in the middle of the West End for an hour, off our heads, before we could get a taxi to pick us up. Finally, one cabbie recognised us and stopped. The crowd at Iron Maiden loved it. So did Ozzy. He adored making that sort of impression and when he'd had a lot to drink, he was on another planet. He led his life like that. He was a madman, a real nutcase, but a lovely bloke. The truth is that Ozzy wouldn't hurt a fly – a chicken maybe, but not a fly. He now lives in a three-million-pound house in LA, but he still talks and acts like he's on an estate in Birmingham. He's excellent. A true star.

When we came back from the States, we were still con-tracted to RCA. For the next couple of years, we continued making records, but things didn't improve. We had a Top 10 hit with a song called 'All Join Hands', but that was about it. The four of us were seeing each other less and we were all pulling in different directions. Jim wanted more control in the studio. Meanwhile, Dave had started writing his own songs and he was miffed that we weren't recording many of them. I thought his songs were good, but the record company didn't agree. If we didn't use them, Dave didn't get writing royalties, so it became a big issue.

We were also having problems with producers. We continued working for a while with John Punter, who had done 'My Oh My' and 'Run Runaway' and the album *Rogues' Gallery*. Then RCA suggested we get in an English guy called Thomas Baker, who lived in America, to work on our next album, *You Boyz Make Big Noize*. He had produced Queen, among others, and was a big name in the early '80s. We flew him and his engineer over from the States. The idea was that he would produce five tracks on the album and Jim would produce the other five. Before we started, we told him exactly what we wanted – our old raucous sound, but with '80s technology. He agreed. Then he spent the first four days in the studio miking up drums. He had twenty-two mics just on Don's kit. He had them on the ceiling, on the floor, everywhere. He was working at a snail's pace, which wasn't our way at all. After two weeks, he had used up nearly our whole budget and he hadn't even finished one song. In the end I had to call a halt. Dave and Don couldn't afford to spend that sort of money on recording. Jim didn't mind because he and this guy had become mates and were going out at night together which didn't help matters. In the end, Thomas Baker did just two tracks. Neither of them was up to scratch. Even RCA thought so and it had been their idea in the first place. We were forced to re-mix them and had to finish the rest of the album ourselves in next to no time and with what was left of the budget. Never again!!

I told the others that I'd had enough. I said I wanted to try other things. They weren't very happy. Don wasn't interested in touring either, but Dave and Jim wanted to carry on. I couldn't believe it. They were the two who moaned the most whenever we were on the road. I said, 'Why don't I leave and you can get another singer? Loads of bands do it. That way, you can carry on for as long as you like.' I didn't want to force anyone else out of a job. As it happened, that was the end for all of us. No one seemed keen to keep the band going and our contract with RCA was already up, so we just wound Slade down.

We never officially said that Slade had split. We left the door open in case anything of interest came up in the future, but we all intended to go off and do our own thing. In 1983, Jim and I produced an album in London for the band Girlschool. It was called *Play Dirty*. It was a good record, but a nightmare to make. The girls just turned up when they felt like it and even then sometimes they'd disappear without warning to go shopping. We had to get a car to pick them up in the morning, then literally lock them in the studio for the rest of the day. They were great fun though. It seemed to us that all they were concerned with was drinking, shagging and getting as much dope down their necks as they could . . . oh, and playing the odd tune. When they did knuckle down to work, they were a good band. It was just that work didn't come too high up on their list of priorities.

I started doing advertising work. I wrote some music for ads, but mainly I sang and did voiceovers. I did one for Pepsi in America. Then I got into radio, which was something I had wanted to do for a while. I was standing in for one of the jocks on a BBC station, when Paul Lockitt, a producer at Piccadilly Radio in Manchester, heard me and asked if I would do a one-off '70s special. That went really well, so he gave me my own six-week series. I've been there ever since. I present a soul show and a '70s show now. I moved from the Midlands to Manchester, partly for my TV and radio work but mainly to be near my kids, who were based there.

The next dealings I had with Slade were in 1991. Polydor still released most of our back catalogue and they wanted to bring out a TV-advertised *Greatest Hits* album. They asked if we would record two new songs and release one of them as a single. Both Jim and Dave had been recording and releasing their own records. I had even sung on one of Dave's records with his new band. I did it as a favour because we were still mates. It was a cover of an Everly Brothers song called 'Crying In The Rain' and it was this that had prompted Polydor's interest.

The four of us decided to record two new songs for the *Greatest Hits* album. The problem was which ones. Jim had one called 'Radio Wall Of Sound' that Polydor really liked, so we went with that. He had another called 'Universe', which was very orchestral, backed by strings and totally unlike anything we had ever done before as Slade. I liked 'Universe', just because it was so different. Dave put a few of his songs forward too and Polydor agreed to put them on the B-sides. When we went into the studio to record 'Radio Wall Of Sound', I had to split the vocals with Jim. They weren't in my key at all. I did the chorus and Jim sang the verses. It was a minor hit, because it got a bit of radio play

– stations love songs with the word radio in the title. Then we brought out 'Universe'. It bombed. It was too far from what people expected of us. That was the last thing we ever did together as Slade.

Dave and Don went on to form Slade 2 with new musicians. I've still never seen them play. I'm not bothered about it. It doesn't really interest me. At first, Jim wanted to stop them using the name. He said it was a slur on the original band.

The first time Dave, Jim, Don and I were in a room together for years was at Chas' funeral in 1996. His death was a real shock. I had seen him only a month earlier at my fiftieth birthday party and he was fine. He had had a bad heart attack a few years earlier. I went to see him in hospital in Newcastle and he was unrecognisable. He was really skinny and terribly ill. We didn't think he was going to survive that, but he did. He went back to his old size and his old self. I sat up all night with him after my birthday party, just chatting. We had a great time. A month later, he was dead. He had just been back to hospital for some tests on his heart and they had passed him okay. He died right after that. All four of us went to his funeral and I was asked to say a few words. The church was packed with all his old buddies. I've stood on stage in front of tens of thousands of people and not thought twice about it. Making that speech was one of the hardest things I've ever had to do. I told a mad story about Chas and us in The Miyako Hotel one night in San Francisco when he'd walked through a paper wall. I didn't want to be solemn, because Chas wasn't that sort of bloke.

The last time I saw Dave, Don and Jim together was a few months after that, when I was caught for *This Is Your Life*. We got on fine, although I didn't see that much of them that night. I had no idea I was to be done by Michael Aspel. My family and friends had all been sworn to secrecy. I thought I was appearing on *Mrs Merton's Christmas Show*. I know Caroline Aherne and my partner Suzan had suggested I

227

could be one of Mrs Merton's guests as the set-up. When I got to the BBC, the floor manager met me at the door of the studio and asked if I'd do a quick walk-on rehearsal before I went to get ready. I hadn't even had a chance to change out of my scraggy clothes and into a suit. He told me to walk through these two big doors on to the stage. I thought it was strange, because the studio was awfully quiet. Suddenly, I saw all these people. I thought, 'Bloody hell, some idiot has let the audience in early.' Then Michael Aspel appeared from behind me. I was gobsmacked. Usually, when they do a hit, people have two or three hours to calm down before the show starts. I went straight to the dressing room, changed, downed a double vodka and I was on.

That was a fantastic night. There were people there who I hadn't seen for years. I had a real cross-section of guests. The showbiz lot included Roy Wood, Brian May, Samantha Janus, Vic Reeves and Bob Mortimer, Gary Glitter, Suzi Quatro, Toyah, Alan Freeman, Keith Chegwin and Mark and Lard from Radio 1. Ozzy was supposed to come, but he missed his plane from LA.

Vic and Bob told a great story when they came on. Everyone thought they were making it up, but it was true. It happened the night I went to see them live in Manchester. Afterwards, Vic, Bob and I went for a drink in The Britannia Hotel. We were walking through the revolving doors into the bar when suddenly this pair of legs came through the ceiling. It was like one of their sketches. This bloke had fallen through the floor up to his waist and his legs were dangling down between the revolving doors. We later found out that he was on a stag night and someone had locked him in a broom cupboard. He was really claustrophobic and he had panicked so much that he had kicked his way through the floor.

Bob also told a story about Alex Higgins threatening to beat him up, that happened that same night. He was in the bar and he got really angry because Bob wouldn't buy him a drink. It's no wonder. He'd been insulting Bob all night for no reason, then he started insisting that he buy him a drink. I've known Alex for twenty years, so I had to step in and sort it out. Alex is nice as pie when he's sober, but very obnoxious when he's pissed. The audience thought they were making these stories up, but they really happened.

I did Vic and Bob's *Shooting Stars* show on TV. I was even in the original pilot. They also did a Slade piss-take every week on their BBC TV series *The Smell of Reeves and Mortimer* in the mid '90s. They sent me the tapes before it went out to find out what I thought. I thought it was hilarious. It was quite near the mark actually. It was an exaggerated version, but still a lot like how we were with each other. Our accents, the way we talked to one another and constantly took the piss was us spot on. The funniest episode was when they put a can on Dave's head and cut his hair. That's how his hair always looked like it had been cut. Then they did Slade on holiday for the second series. Great stuff. Two of the most original comics ever.

A couple of years ago, Oasis gave one of our songs a new lease of life when they covered 'Cum On Feel The Noize'. I was surprised when I heard they wanted to do a Slade song, but I suppose it did fit their style of music. They did a great version. When they played at Maine Road stadium in Manchester, they invited me to go and see them. They did 'Cum On Feel The Noize' as the encore that night. It was a real buzz for me seeing 40,000 kids of their generation going berserk over a song I co-wrote twenty years before.

I know we've been a big influence on a lot of young bands. When some of them come to do interviews at the radio station in Manchester, they see me and tell me how they used to buy our records or what Slade songs they like best. In recent years, we've had bands all over the world cover our stuff. A Canadian group called Bran Van 3000 recently did 'Cum On Feel The Noize'. It was fantastic, totally different from our version, really off the wall. Last year, a French band covered 'Merry Xmas Everybody' in the style of Les Negresses Vertes. I like it when musicians make an effort to change the song, to make it their own. It's fascinating for me to hear them.

My parents always found it hard to understand my success with Slade. I don't think my mum realised I was famous until I was on *This Is Your Life*, although she and all my aunties were more over the moon with meeting Michael Aspel than anything else. My mum was eighty then. My dad was no longer with us. He died in the late '80s. It wasn't sudden. He was in hospital for months. He had a load of things wrong with him. He'd suffered a couple of mild heart attacks, he had diabetes and he had bad arthritis from doing the windows in all weather. He and my mum only saw me play once with Slade after we became famous. It was at a gig in Wolverhampton in 1973. They had heard about us from people they knew and seen us on TV, but they didn't have any idea how popular we were. They had never been to a rock concert in their lives. The size of the show, the lights, the volume of the music and the crowd reaction was a big shock for them.

My mum and dad could never relate to me being the person that they saw on stage that night. I could tell that when I saw them the next day. They hadn't turned up to the aftershow party and their attitude to me had changed. Until then, they still hoped that I would pack the band in and get a proper job. Suddenly, they understood what I had been doing all those years, although they couldn't really get their heads around it.

My mum is eighty-three now. She still lives in the same house on the estate where I grew up. She's been there forty-five years. The area is all built up now, of course. There are no longer fields or pools to go fishing in. It's a tough inner-city area, but mum doesn't want to move. My dad never did either. Mum is comfortable there. She has all her close friends nearby and my dad's sister is a neighbour. They go to the bingo together and look after each other if one of them is ill. I couldn't uproot her from that.

I still live in Manchester. I share a house on the outskirts of the city with my partner, Suzan, who is a TV producer. We've been together for most of the '90s and we have a five-year-old son called Django. I never thought I'd be a dad again in my late forties, but it's great. I get to do all the things with Django that I wasn't around for with my other kids.

I don't miss Slade. I did for a while, but it seems so far in the past now. I've been too busy doing other things to think much about it. I have my own pop quiz show called *Noddy's Electric Ladyland* and Keith Chegwin, Toyah and I had a series on satellite TV called *Roll With It*.. I've done adverts for Bank's Beer, Asda, Young's Fish and Cadburys, which I enjoy a lot.

After over thirty years working in rock 'n' roll bands, it's now interesting and exciting to be doing different things each day. I could be in the radio or TV studio one day, doing the voice of Dudley Sidebottom for Cadbury's the next, or sitting in the caravan on location waiting to film a scene for *The Grimley's* alongside Brian Conley as he shows me the 'No Entry' tattoo on his backside!

Recently I've been filming a second series of the TV comedy-drama set in Dudley during the mid 1970s. The writer Jed Mercurio captures the mood of the Black Country so perfectly, it makes me homesick. My role as the music teacher calls for me to perform some of Slade's classics in different styles. I've been approached by record companies to do an album of solo acoustic versions, but I wouldn't do just Slade songs.

Who knows what the future holds? I've had a good time so far and it's impossible to cram all the stories into the one book. Watch this space.

And Keep On Rockin'!